Chinism and New Pragmatism

How China's Development Success and
Innovative Economic Thinking Contribute
to the Global Development

Grzegorz W. Kolodko

Prunus Press USA

Chinism and New Pragmatism

How China's Development Success and Innovative
Economic Thinking Contribute to the Global Development

Copyright © China National Publications Import and Export
(Group) Co., Ltd.

Written by Grzegorz W. Kolodko

Edited by Richard ZHAO

Designed by Brandy Ding

First Edition 2022

ISBN: 978-1-61612-151-8

Prunus Press USA

Contents

Part II The Great Chinese Transformation: from the Third to the First World

Introduction

Nowadays, there is not only a day, but also even an hour, for global news agencies not to refer to what is happening in China. This is of interest to the enormity of people in all corners of the rapidly changing world, the more so as the phenomena and processes taking place in China have a significant and increasingly noticeable impact on what is happening in other countries. Some admire China, others fear it. While some watch it closely and wish for further achievements, others look enviously and hope that the unrestrained progress of the past four decades will stop. While some see China as an opportunity for a more inclusive nature of irreversible globalization, others fear that it may dominate the world.

It is obvious that the basis of China's globalization is unprecedented social and economic development. Nobody has ever achieved so much for so many in such a short time and nobody will repeat in the future similar success on such a scale. For other reasons, economic and political, this was achieved in the past, especially in 1987-2021; for other reasons, political and ecological, there will be no such scale of production and consumption growth in any country in the future.

China's economic success was possible thanks to a specific system that I refer to as Chinism. It is a unique combination of the power of the state, with its structures and the visible leaders, and the market, with its institutions and the invisible hand. The synergy of these two super-regulators of the economy, society and polity, combined with meritocracy, when rational people make rational decisions in a rational way, made a historical leap of civilization possible.

Chinism may seem like an attractive recipe for the development of other countries looking for their own roads towards a better future. Perhaps not one of them will follow a similar path in the sphere of capital accumulation and its effective allocation – those foundations for the healthy functioning of the economy and its growth. However, it must be remembered that the synergy of the state and the market inherent in Chinism alone is not enough. Its cultural environment and embedding it in social relations are also important. In these respects, in many cases it is impossible to replicate what the Chinese can do – with their inherent discipline, the capacity to work as a team, and the ability to look at the long future distance. Moreover, other countries – if they want to learn from the experience and achievements of Chinism – must know that the effectiveness of macro-economic policy and micro-economic management depends not only on the quality of state and market institutions, but also on culture, social cohesion, and above all the quality of human capital, to which extent China has also made a huge leap in recent years. This time it was a constructive great leap forward...

I am a university economist, although I have extensive experience in economic practice gained while managing economic policy in Poland as Deputy Prime Minister and Minister of Finance in four governments in the 1990s and 2000s. As a scientist and researcher, I have always focused my theoretical studies on economic challenges, primarily in the fields of macroeconomic policy and development strategy. In the modern world one cannot seriously discuss these fundamental issues apart from globalization. Moreover, it is impossible to think about both, development of the world economy, without an intellectual effort to understand what is happening in China and why is it happening there – the most populous country in the world with already the largest, greater than the American economy (counting production and consumption according to the purchasing power parity, PPP).

This research led me to outline the theory of New Pragmatism. It is a theoretic, yet strongly oriented towards economic policy, a heterodox concept of triple sustainable development: economically, socially and ecologically. China has already achieved a lot in this regard, but there is still much to be done, especially in terms of reducing income inequalities and enhancing social cohesion, as well as environmental protection and creating a green economy.

The New Pragmatism is not the same as Chinism, but there is no doubt that the economic policies pursued over the last few decades – domestic and foreign, investment and trade, financial and monetary – largely derive from this theoretical trend. That is one more reason encouraging me to participate so intensely in professional debates taking place in China and all over the world about the Chinese phenomenon. I participate in various scientific conferences and give lectures at various universities too, regularly in the Belt and Road School at Beijing Normal University, where I am a Distinguished Professor. I give often media interviews and I do publish a lot of research papers and numerous books on the matters relevant to China, globalization, and development[1].

Therefore, I begin this book with a concise overview of the essence of New Pragmatism, and then share my interpretation and assessment of the Chinese development process, paying attention, on the one hand, to its determinants and, on the other, to the consequences

---

1. Vide the lists of my publications in the Chinese language and the works on China published in the English language at the end of the book.

and implications for other countries and for the world economy. Its future will increasingly depend on China's future. Writing about the future, I naturally refer to the development challenges that China will face in the decade of 2020s and beyond. I believe that the Chinese society, its political leaders, and intellectual and professional elites are fully aware of these challenges, but it is always worth discussing them in a matter-of-fact way. This is also the message of this short book.

Part I

Economics of New Pragmatism:
Identity, Aims, Method

| Introduction

Modern economic thought does not deal suitably with the tasks it faces. Neither does it provide a satisfactory explanation of the socio-economic reality, nor does it propose effective methods of solving the mounting problems, especially at the macroeconomic level, in the national economy, and in the mega-economic level, in the world economy. The beyond-GDP reality, in which we are already for some time, requires a beyond-GDP economic theory on which a triple balanced – economically, socially and ecologically – beyond-GDP development strategy must be based. It is necessary to formulate anew the goal of economic activity, which cannot be a simple maximization of profit and a quantitative increase in production. The short-term interests of private capital should be subordinated to the long-term public interests, which is to be fostered by appropriate reinstitutionalization of the market economy. The economics has to be more and more oriented towards addressing the future challenges, and not mainly be inspired by conclusions from observations of past events, which is often of little use in economic policy. The enormity of changes taking place in technology, economy, society, culture and the natural environment forces us to abandon orthodox economics and look for innovative economic thought. This necessity is met by new pragmatism – the outline of an eclectic, interdisciplinary theory of economics focused on future-oriented economic policy.

Economics is a beautiful science because it serves human well-being. It is knowledge about economic activity in all its aspects, and when we are able to add further, new observations of phenomena and processes and their innovative theoretical explanations for the knowledge accumulated over generations, it is more than just knowledge – it is a science. Nevertheless, it remains a science for as long as it is at the service of truth, when it focuses on objective analyses and in-depth generalizations, and not when it becomes ugly, when it is merely an instrument in the constantly ongoing political and ideological quarrels or a tool in the hands of lobbyists of special interest groups. In these two cases, economic knowledge is undoubtedly useful, but it is not a science; and by no means, this type of activities cannot be assigned the attributes of beauty inherent to economics as a science that perceives and examines human behavior – individual, group, social, civilizational – and expresses its interpretations in theoretical frames. One can therefore speak of economics as a science when it creates value added in terms of the knowledge about economic activity.

However, the matter gets complicated because not only there are unresolved problems, but also economics itself is in a phase of fundamental changes. According to many authors, economics is in the throes of a crisis (Skidelsky, 2020), and some even claim that it is a broken science, believing at the same time – like *Alice in Wonderland* – in various contradictions (Cooper, 2014). Indeed, economics is currently in a quite difficult situation, which results, on the one hand, from the essence of the investigated matter, meaning the condition of the modern economy and its cultural, political and technological environment, and, on the other hand, from the functions which the advanced and enriched knowledge about economic activity is to perform. From both of these points of view, the present period is special, as it raises new questions to which new answers have to be sought. This is a fascinating challenge that traditional schools of economic thought cannot successfully tackle. A different reality requires a different approach to it.

Identity of economics

With the constant movement of people, goods and services they produce and provide, economic thought wanders as well – together with the accompanying questions and answers. For some time now – counted using decades and generations rather than years and political electoral cycles – we have been living in the world of a new quality, which from a broad economic perspective can be described as a beyond-GDP reality. This implies the need to develop a beyond-GDP economic theory that will serve as the base for a beyond-GDP economic policy and a beyond-GDP development strategy addressing the current and future problems. The beyond-GDP reality means that many economic phenomena and processes, *sensu largo*, occur beyond the fields of activity observed and explained by the existing traditional economic thought, which has focused on studying the conditions and mechanisms of growth, identified, in simple terms, with the maximization of return on the invested capital on a micro scale, and with the maximization of the national income, most often understood as a gross domestic product, GDP, on a macro scale.

Today's economics describes and interprets a considerably different economy and society than with what Adam Smith did when he announced *An Inquiry into the Nature and Causes of the Wealth of Nations* in 1776. He could describe the sphere of production as viewed through the prism of a pin factory and barter relations based on contracts between a baker and a shoemaker. Now, this must be done, *inter alia*, by analyzing global financial flows and distribution relationships in the on-line sector. Of course, bakers and shoemakers are still needed, although the uncritical apologists of hi-tech feel that this is no longer the case; that a smartphone, Spotify, and Uber will do the job, that it's enough just to click. The GDP per capita in England back then (Smith did not yet know this category; it was a before-GDP economy) was about 15 times lower than it is today, while the population of the economically loosely connected world – producing, on average, *per capita*, as much as the English – was about 10 times less numerous than it is now. Thus, the whole world produced some 150 times less than it does nowadays. Forty years later, although the economy has already gained momentum as a result of the Industrial Revolution, which, in time, we have called the first, and humankind has already exceeded the first billion, David Ricardo studied international trade relations and developed the theory of comparative costs by analyzing the exchange of English cloth for Portuguese wine.

Today's economy is also very different from the one described and interpreted by Karl Marx in *Capital* one and a half century ago because over time more sophisticated ways of getting rich at the expense of others have emerged than the primitive and brutal 19th century exploitation of the working class by the bourgeoisie. Our economy is also different from the one intellectually embraced three generations later by John Maynard Keynes, explaining the demand-side mechanisms for controlling the economy on a macroeconomic scale. The breakthrough he made in economic thought was no longer sufficient half a century later as a result of the intensification of the modern phase of globalization, that is, the liberalization and integration of the national economies and capital, goods, and labor markets, previously functioning to some extent isolated, into one interconnected global market. The previous misconception in that the sum of microeconomic rationalities (if any) does not make up the macroeconomic rationality, which Keynesian interventionism tried to correct, was exacerbated by the second-generation misconception where the sum of macroeconomic rationalities (if any) in no way makes up the global rationality.

The memorable contribution to the science of economics of Smith, Ricardo, Marx, and Keynes, as well as many other important scholars, cannot be overstated. However, there is no doubt that if they were faced with the reality given to us, they would formulate other, sometimes completely different questions and come to different conclusions with what they did in their times. This is indirectly demonstrated by the later achievements of such economic theorists as Friedrich Hayek, Gunnar Myrdal, Simon Kuznets, Milton Friedman, John Kenneth Galbraith, Paul Samuelson, Gerard Debreu, Douglass North, Janos Kornai or Joseph Stiglitz, and in Poland Oskar Lange and Michał Kalecki.

The evolution of the research field of economics about a post-industrial economy that happened over the past half-century has also quickly proved to be insufficient. This is supported by the fact that economics is not able to answer numerous and salient questions if it disregards such categories as expectations, irrationality, the value of leisure time, the price of fresh air, social cohesion, complexity, or geopolitics. However, investigating the conflicts of economic interests and suggesting ways to resolve them still remain the backbone of economics. There is no economics without conflicts of interests. We also constantly have to deal with the differences between our ideas (Brunnermeier, James and Landau, 2016). It is sometimes the case that even where there are obvious contradictions, economists, moving on the solid grounds of reality rather than strolling around in Wonderland, can prove the validity of opposing views. It is a bit like in an old joke when a curious young man asks an old wise man:

"How much is two times two?" and receives the answer "Well, it depends if you're selling or buying…"

In the beyond-GDP reality, the core of the conflict of economic interests and ideas is different than it used to be, which is a natural consequence of the advance of productive forces and the evolution of production relations. Such trends as institutional, behavioral, experimental economics or neuro-economics have contributed a great deal to the study of changes that are taking place, but it is necessary to go further, deeper and broader, and above all, to make economic thinking more prospective. If economics is not able to stay ahead of the forthcoming processes, let it at least keep up with them. If modern economics cannot be the economics of tomorrow, let it at least not be the economics of yesterday.

Contemporary economics in its research must go beyond the area of the market, even in its broadest sense, sometimes delving into the nooks and crannies of human thought processes, and sometimes into the interactions taking place in the triad of "economy – society – state". Actually, the Clinton slogan "It's the economy, stupid" – this very popular, yet coined by chance, phrase of Bill Clinton's presidential campaign of 1992 – is a sort of neo-Marxist claim that the social being determines the consciousness of men, that the material base governs the physical and cultural condition of the society. Now we also know that it is sometimes the consciousness that determines social being, and it certainly has a huge impact on it. Additionally, there is the state that participates in shaping these relations, and in the era of globalization, also international and global regulations take part.

The condition of the economy is so complex that economic thought – theorizing about its purpose, content, and method – needs to be pushed into new directions. It certainly has to leave the current mainstream of thought for good because the resulting models have moved too far away from the realities of economic life. American academic jargon speaks of two schools of economics: the one of the leading universities of the East and West Coast (Columbia, Harvard, MIT, Princeton, Yale, Berkeley, Stanford and UCLA) and the other of the universities of the Great Lakes Region (Carnegie Mellon, Chicago, Michigan, Urbana-Champaign, Minnesota and Rochester). Referring to their dominance in the promoted economic theories, rightly with some intellectual skepticism, James Kenneth Galbraith writes about the option in the form of backwater economics (Galbraith, 2018), because indeed, many precious thoughts emerge over other waters. It is the same case outside the USA(Csaba, 2009; Lin, 2012b and 2013; Nuti, 2018; Piatkowski, 2018; Tirole, 2017). What textbooks contain does not cover what is actually happening in reality, and science cannot ignore and over-simplify it.

The world, inhabited by nearly eight billion people producing a gross product of more than USD 130 trillion (calculated according to purchasing power parity, PPP) and creating plenty of economic and social problems, is structurally unbalanced, thus generating conflicts, even reaching the breaking point. While there are authors who argue that the situation is not bad at all (Milanovic, 2019; Ridley, 2010, Rosling and Ronnlund, 2018), others claim that the world and civilization are facing a meltdown. While some outline almost catastrophic visions, and certainly do not see any sensible future for capitalism (Harvey, 2015), others are convinced that this can be rectified by fundamental changes (Acemoglu and Robinson, 2012; King, 2013; Kolodko, 2014a; Phelps, 2013; Stiglitz, 2019a). If a rising tide cannot lift all boats, also those of the little ones, then at least let it not be the case that many of them sink and only yachts are lifted, mostly the luxurious ones.

Over the next few years, we will hear more often – as we already hear – about the end of the world as we know it, about the collapse of the market economy, about post-capitalism, again about the third way and socialism; new terms will appear, such as the digital economy, sharing economy (Sundararajan, 2017), gig economy based on digital platforms (Kessler, 2018), or Chinism (Kolodko, 2018); the old will return with determiners such as "new" or "neo" added as in new nationalism (*Economist*,

2016) or in new authoritarianism (Wiatr, 2019), or with the adjective "true", as in true progressivism[2]. The concepts known from the past, such as ordoliberalism and the social market economy, will revive. The new-old categories will be preventively criticized, as was the case with the collective capitalism accused of being deprived of two attributes of a healthy economy: responsibility for deciding what people need and dynamism (*Economist*, 2019a), or the welfare state which is claimed to entail excessive fiscalism and an excessive, from the point of view of efficiency, redistribution of income.

As a result, the first thing that will prevail – as it is already doing so – is the conceptual noise and definitional clutter. Yet, in time, some sort of compact concept of a new socio-economic system, or rather new systems, may emerge because with all its consequences for the economic sciences, there will be no more uniformity. Just like, in practice, it has never been there in the past; it has occurred only in some theoretical models simplifying reality.

---

2. Shortly after the outbreak of the financial crisis of 2008, chances were being sought to save the unstable neoliberal capitalism by its evolution towards "True Progressivism" (*Economist*, 2012). This notion does not disappear, by no means. Interestingly, it appeared next to two other terms in the name of a scientific conference – "Progressivism, Socialism, Nationalism" – organized in September 2019 at the Columbia University in New York by the Centre on Capitalism and Society, headed by the Nobel Prize winner, Edmund Phelps (vide https://capitalism.columbia.edu/17th-annual-conference-progressivism-socialism-nationalism;).

Hence, we are now living in the era, when a new reality is being formed, and a new system that is different from the previous ones has to be intellectually embraced, understood, and explained. Ways to influence its evolution need to be proposed to allow for the co-formation of its desired shape. It is clear that there will be constant axiological disputes – and they are already going on – concerning its shape, and that its appearance will be a function of resolving conflicts of ideas and interests that are piling up. Humanity is not doomed to some predetermined future; there is no determinism. This future can and must be shaped. Given that the answer to the question of how to do this needs to be constantly sought, economics has a good future ahead of it.

Terminological rigor is very important in the scientific debate, as many of the disputes arise because the interlocutors who present their arguments do not mean the same thing. How to resolve the dispute over whether there is a "state capitalism" (Roland, 2019), or corrupt "crony capitalism" (Minxin, 2016) in China or, as the Chinese leaders prefer, "socialism with Chinese characteristics," if, when sticking to the definitions proposed by the authors, in one and the same reality, each of these systems is present there? Is democracy in Poland still liberal or no longer liberal? Because in Hungary it is already illiberal (Csaba, 2019)? Does the market economy in Turkey and Russia operate in the political environment of a democratic or autocratic system? While some authors use different terms to describe the same reality, others refer to different realities using the same term. It happens therefore that after a thorough explanation of the terms used the subject matter of the dispute or the source of the political conflict disappears. All the more, a continuous substantive dialogue is needed.

So, what kind of economics are we talking about? What is it supposed to analyze and interpret? Whether, and if so, what and how should it propose to change for the better? This is astonishing because although it would seem that the economic knowledge accumulated over the centuries should provide easy and consensual answers to these questions, it often becomes helpless when faced with the accumulating challenges. It happens so for at least two reasons. Firstly, due to the enormous qualitative diversity of the realities studied, economics is becoming a more and more contextual science while universal laws apply to a lesser degree. Secondly, economic thought often fails to keep pace with the rapidly changing reality. A Marxist would say that observations, analyses, and generalizations are not keeping pace with evolving production relationships, which are being overwhelmingly influenced by the rapidly changing nature of production forces. An institutionalist would conclude that the rules of the market game remain in discord with the rapid changes taking place in technology and the organization of production and exchange.

Objectives of economics

Humanity is facing epochal challenges. Meeting them forces lifestyle changes, with which the operation of the economy different than it used to be must be correlated. In turn, all this determines the need to redefine the objective of economic activity. These epochal challenges stem from overlapping seven mega-trends that are significant for the contemporary times:

1. demographic changes, especially the aging of the population and the huge variations in fertility rates,
2. environmental changes, especially the depletion of non-renewable resources and global warming,
3. the scientific and technological revolution, especially the digitization of the economy and culture, as well as automation,
4. non-inclusive globalization, especially increasing areas of exclusion and inequality,
5. the general crisis of neoliberal capitalism, especially the structural economic imbalance,
6. the crisis of liberal democracy, especially the accompanying polarization of societies, rise of populism and new authoritarianism, the Second Cold War, especially the escalation of US-China

tensions.

So, capitalism does not get along with itself. Even such an excellent supporter as the British-American opinion leading weekly, *The Economist*, had to notice that "in the West, capitalism is not working as well as it should be" (*Economist*, 2019a). It is not working because it cannot, as it is experiencing a structural crisis (Bremmer, 2010; Galbraith, 2014; Stiglitz, 2019b). The lack of fair competition, bad regulation, corruption of politicians and bureaucracy; the self-interest of business and financial elites; such extent of greed and avarice that the best business schools have taught that greed is good; fraud by manufacturers, distributors and service providers, starting from the banking sector, through the automotive sector, ending with the pharmaceutical sector (Akerlof and Shiller, 2015); driving up consumerism gouging capitalist profits; corrupt media manipulating public opinion; cynicism of the political elites – all these had to reap a bitter harvest.

Capitalism, contaminated by market fundamentalism, without changing its essence, i.e. its system of values and fundamental principles, may not survive the current historical turn. This is as interesting as it is difficult and dangerous because tons of questions immediately emerge. What's next? In return for what? If indeed post-capitalism, then of what sort? What are the desired changes if all that remains is to escape forward? Because there is not much to go back to. Old technologies cannot be used to raise a new building on a new planet. Moreover, the Earth of the 21st century is an utterly different planet from that of previous centuries.

While analyzing the various economic systems and determining their efficiency features, we are led to the conclusion that they are not equivalent in an axiological sense. Moreover, even within the same economic system, there are better and worse economies. A good economy is capable of a long-term and harmonious development that maintains the proper relationship between the present and the future. What people need is not an economy in general, but a good economy. Economic activity cannot be isolated from the values that it is supposed to serve. On the path of history, the notion of good and bad in the economy, and – because it is not the same – good and bad economy, has profoundly changed (Sedlacek, 2011). Today, we are closer not only to categories such as profitability and justice, but also social cohesion and solidarity, generational responsibility and environmental awareness.

A good economy must be efficient and competitive, but these are only the means that should not be confused with the objective of meeting the needs. The good economy calls for a good policy. The good policy is to give people not what they want but what they need. This is the imperative of the economy of moderation, which is described by the economics of moderation and which the economics of moderation is intended to serve. This is not about usurpers forcing consumption patterns and lifestyles invented by them, but about affecting these patterns and lifestyles in a public, democratic discourse. It must be responsible and based on scientific findings that say what is objectively healthy and beneficial individually and socially. Thus, real politics is not only supposed to capture social preferences accurately but also to stimulate them sensibly. A good upbringing and education, as well as the social impact on desirable consumption patterns from the point of view of sustainable development and improved welfare, must therefore consist of shaping consumption preferences in such a way that people want what serves them well as often as possible. The vast amount of knowledge provided by behavioral economics (Kahneman, 2011; Thaler, 2016; Thaler and Sunstein, 2009) facilitates work in this field. Unfortunately, the knowledge is effectively used for the opposing purpose (Kuenzler, 2017). What is missing is the sufficient political determination to go in the right direction (Kolodko, 2014b; Krugman, 2020).

In recent decades, much damage has been done to economic thought by neoliberal economics, which makes a few illusory assumptions. The first of these is that the market operates under the conditions of full competition. To some extent, it always does but never under perfect competition because markets are largely oligopolistic – from large retail chains and airlines through banks and insurance agencies to pharmaceutical companies and social media. Indeed, the pressure of the neoliberal circles for deregulation consists in demanding – and often obtaining – the legislation they want, not so much to deepen the competitive environment but rather to make it easier for them to maximize their own benefits from rent seeking. Not once or twice does deregulation come down to making it easier to cut out relatively weaker competitors inconvenient for the stronger companies. In many cases, this is fostered by a hypocritical policy that preaches one thing and does something else. This must be changed, and the way to do this is to introduce regulations towards a social market economy and to take into account the interests of medium-sized and small enterprises and their stakeholders.

The rationality of economic entities, both businesses and households, is also insufficient. The rational one is the one who acts for its own benefit, given the information. Assuming for a moment that people think and know what is good for them in their various economic roles – and if they do not know, then they know where and from whom they can find it out (Sloman and Fernbach, 2017) – the information is decisive. There is often an asymmetry here – an imbalance in favor of the generally better-informed producers and merchants. The position of buyers and consumers *sensu largo* is weaker. It is deliberately further aggravated by the forces manipulating buyers and misinforming them through marketing and advertising so that, thinking that they are acting for their own benefit, and actually provide income and generate profits to someone else. Then they harm themselves when compared to a hypothetical optimization of behavior if they were provided with full and balanced information.

The commanding forces of the triad: power – capital – information (or, in other words: politics – money – media) often act so to make people irrational in the market. It is the power of the civil state – with its market regulation – to counteract this. The market, even if it was fully competitive, would never solve this syndrome by itself. Here, educational and institutional state intervention is needed. It is the responsibility of the state. Freedom is indeed about the ability to make choices, but genuine freedom only exists if the voters – here buyers and consumers – are fairly informed about what they are buying and consuming.

An immense effort must be made to create a proper institutional set-up for the market in order to bring the realities of the modern market economy as close as possible to the ideal of full competition, with sufficient information provided to the entities pursuing economic activity. Without progress in this field, consumer sovereignty will also be illusory. Its condition *sine qua non* is to be aware of the options to choose from and the associated marginal utility. The directions of the necessary structural reforms in these areas require a fundamental systemic and political strengthening of public authorities supervising fair competition and protecting consumer interests. It is right that actions are being taken to this end both in the United States and in the European Union, although less right is that their authorities seem to be more willing to impose penalties, sometimes worth billions of euros, on competitive companies on the other side of the ocean.

There is no global economy without national economies; there are no national economies without a microeconomic sphere. There is no macroeconomics without microeconomics. What, then, are the microeconomic foundations for innovative economics that would meet the upcoming challenges? It is clear that the economy must continue to rely on the dominance of private companies, except that their functioning and expansion must be regulated by the state in the general interest. The aim of an entrepreneur remains to maximize the rate of return on the capital employed, which the state is supposed to encourage with a proper institutional set-up. At the same time, the state is supposed to make it more difficult for an entrepreneur to drive up its own profits through rent seeking – exploitation of stakeholders and passing on some of the incurred costs on them, as well as capturing income earned by someone else in the various phases and channels of distribution. The state with the proper market regulation, with the concern about the circulation of information and the fight against disinformation, is to encourage entrepreneurship to flourish and to encourage investment, but still to influence economic activity in such a way that it is consistent with the macroeconomic objective of improving the welfare of the society. Where institutional and politico-economic alignment of the interests of shareholders and stakeholders is possible, this should be done consistently. Good practices in this respect are brought about by ordo liberalism and the social market economy.

Today, an important new element of economic activity is that sometimes access to reliable information is more meaningful to the formation and allocation of capital than that of ownership. This issue has both a technical and a moral dimension. This makes it even more necessary to strive for reliability in economic activity and high ethical standards in business and economic policy. For the economy to be good, it must be fair, which once again raises the issues of healthy market competition and good state regulation.

It is not possible to eliminate the aforementioned

misconceptions, but they can be mitigated as much on the micro-macro level (enterprises – national economy) as on the macro-mega level (national economy – global economy). Again, without the state in the first case and its transnational agreements between the governments and their proper actions in the second, little can be achieved here. Not only does the market itself fail to solve these problems, but it also intensifies them. However, to move things forward, one must not be fooled by the glittering, but merely verbal, readiness of the private sector to be almost charitable. It is not its purpose. Milton Friedman (1970) was right when he said that corporate social responsibility was about maximizing shareholder value. However, Joseph Stiglitz (2019c) is also right when he says that this responsibility is to pay taxes. In a fair well-regulated economy, one does not exclude the other.

Having been frightened by the wave of populism, chaotic reactions of some politicians, and anti-establishment sentiments, capitalists declare their willingness to look after the interests of others, not just their own. We cannot be easily deceived, because it is nothing more than tactics in the fear of losing one's own powerful position. The statement made by more than 180 top managers of large companies at America's Business Roundtable in August 2019 is not the maximization of shareholder value that is their main objective, but the satisfaction of all stakeholders. It is just pulling the wool over the eyes, which is supposed to push aside the determination of politics to change regulations to such that take more account of social objectives. When a big business – especially the one that has neither clean hands nor clear conscience – heard announcements of the planned systemic changes and revaluations of economic policies by Bernie Sanders and Elizabeth Warren[3] (*Economist*, 2019c), the Democratic contenders for the US Presidency, or Jeremy Corbyn, the left-wing leader of the British Labourists, it was willing to declare almost a transition to quasi-socialist positions (*Economist*, 2019b). For a while, and on paper. Unless…

Unless, indeed, there is another great change coming under the influence of the coincidence of the growing grassroots pressure of significant parts of the society dissatisfied with the state of affairs and the determination of some enlightened political leaders that it should and can be better than before. History knows such cases. Under the growing pressure from the increasingly organized labor movement and the specter of communism that circulated in Europe[4], the capitalism of the late 19th

---

3. Elizabeth Warren accurately diagnoses the fundamental vices of American capitalism (Warren, 2018). She is right to say that this system is corrupt and fails ordinary people. Joseph Stiglitz goes even further in his harsh assessments and shows how deeply corrupt this system is, tolerating exploitation and fraud, and how flawed its policies are (Stiglitz, 2019c).

4. "A spectre is haunting Europe – the spectre of communism", wrote Marx and Engels in the *Communist Manifesto*, first published in 1848.

century became less nasty than that of its beginning, although it was still necessary to fight for a ban on child labor or for an eight-hour working day. Later, in the 1960s, the program of President Lyndon B. Johnson "Great Society" (Zelizer, 2015) was a considerable push for capitalism to new and better tracks. This was due to the coincidence of mass protests against the flagrant injustice expressed in the huge areas of social exclusion, poverty and racial discrimination, on the one hand, and the pressure resulting from the perception of positive examples from the socialist economy characterized by full employment, free health care, universal education, state promotion of culture and safety on the streets, on the other. The progressive changes that were introduced in the United States back then, and which were also followed in some other countries, became permanent over time.

Will it be the same this time too? There are enough protests going on against the unacceptable state of affairs but the actions "Occupy Wall Street" and "Occupy London" widely reported a few years earlier seem to be already forgotten. Are there enough enlightened leaders seeking genuine changes *pro publico bono*? Do they have anything to reach out to? Are there political ideas and programs that are sufficiently attractive but, most importantly, pragmatic? Are there new economic theories on which practical programs can be based? Will it be possible to force them through, breaking the conservatism and resistance of special interest groups? Do we have satisfactory knowledge about the good practices, which at the time of globalization can be spilled over by the science of management? This is a crucial time, and we must be very careful not to be deceived by the hypocrisy of some parts of business and political elites, nor to stray away into the wilderness of populism. If this can be done, capitalism will survive, although perhaps over time it will be of such a new quality that a new term will have to be invented. After all, it definitely is not the end of history. Yet, one has to be very careful because no man can ever step in the same river twice but it is still possible to step twice in the same swamp.

To achieve the redefined objective of economic activity, it is necessary to follow the path of a triple-balanced development – economically, socially, and environmentally. There are feedback loops among these spheres. Now, neither of these balances can be maintained in the long run without the other two. The condition of the classic dynamic economic balance – between production and sales, income and expenditure, savings and investments, imports and exports – even if it is achieved, is no longer sufficient. What is needed is a social balance expressed by a high degree of social cohesion, satisfactory outlays on social capital, and an impassable level of income inequality. A level impassable in both directions, downwards and upwards, is one that favors the formation of capital, on the one hand, and is not contested as being unfair, on the other. What is needed is an ecological balance that enables people to live their everyday life where the water is clean and the grass is green, and that does not deplete natural resources in the long term and does not deprive future generations of access to them. The balance between today and tomorrow is even more difficult to achieve than that between the two sides of traditional balances.

Since we are living in the beyond-GDP economy that operates in a world that is different from before, we need to redefine the purpose of economic activity. On a macro-economic scale, it is prosperity, which is determined not only by the traditional level of consumption of goods and services but also by the quality of the natural, cultural, and political environment in which this consumption occurs. It is becoming increasingly important not *to have*, but *to be*. Even the high level of consumption – and this is still far from being the case for the vast majority of mankind – does not guarantee satisfaction with the economic activity if it is not accompanied by social cohesion and proper moral space.

One goes depending on where one aims. Thus, the metrics of development should be changed so that following them serves the purpose of progress in terms of prosperity. More and more metrics are being proposed (Stiglitz, Fitoussi and Durand, 2019), some only directionally, such as the Integrated Success Index, ISI (Kolodko, 2011), others operationally, such as the Inequality-Adjusted Human Development Index, IHDI, calculated by the United Nations Development Programme, UNDP, or the Better Life Index, BLI, estimated by the Organization for Economic Cooperation and Development, OECD. In the case of composite indices, which also take account of the subjective feelings of the population as regards both their material situation and their cultural and political situation[5], it may happen that even when real incomes are rising, but at the same time moods are pessimistic, the situation is getting worse. This happens when the authorities say that it is getting better and the working and non-working people of cities, towns, and villages think that it is getting worse. As a result, people first fly off the handle and then take to the streets[6].

---

5. Such an index is, *inter alia*, "Legatum Prosperity Index" (https://www.prosperity.com/).

6. Of course, people also take to the streets for other, uneconomical reasons, for example emphasizing that "Black Lives Matter", crying out *Konstytucja*! across Poland, appealing for fully democratic elections to be held in the Московскогог ородскогосовета, singing *Hai Tanahku Papua* during protests in the courtyard of Cenderawasih University in Jayapura, demanding *Catalunya Lliure* at La Rambla in Barcelona, or marching through Avenida 18 de Julio in Montevideo and demanding *Vivir Sin Miedo*.

So it goes in rich countries, as demonstrated by the French case of the wave of demonstrations of so-called yellow vests in response to the increase in excise duty on diesel fuel; in moderately developed countries, such as the vibrant demonstrations in Chile provoked by the increase in the prices of metro tickets in Santiago; or in poor countries such as Ecuador, where the eruption of protests was triggered by the reduction in state subsidies to energy prices. It is interesting and important that in each of these cases, there was an economic and sometimes ecological justification for the price rises, but the social consequences were ignored. In a narrow economic equation, perhaps everything would make sense; in an integrated equation of the economic, social, and environmental balance it is not the case.

This is a wider problem inherent in the essence to the triple balance. Or, unfortunately, more often, to an imbalance. It is caught up in the contradiction between minimizing the costs and risks in one sphere – economic, social, or environmental – and increasing the costs and risks in the other, or in the remaining two (risk-risk trade-off). Traditional economics cannot accurately weigh and compare these costs and accurately estimate and confront these risks. There is much to be done to examine and interpret these relations, above all with reference to economic policy measures and development strategies that promote a comprehensive balance.

These indices show how much the narrative is changing, and even more so how much economic policy would change if it were subordinated to more accurately formulated objectives. While the USA in the ranking by income (GDP per capita according to PPP) is fifth in the OECD (after Luxembourg, Ireland, Norway, and Switzerland), in BLI comparisons, it falls to the 10th position[7]. According to the first criterion, Poland is ranked 31st in this group (between Portugal and Hungary) and 27th according to the second metrics (between Slovakia and Lithuania)[8]. In terms of HDI, which is equally affected by the size of GDP per capita, the state of society's education and its health (one-third by each), and IHDI, which is further adjusted for inequalities, this specific charm of countries compared to their traditional appearance is also sometimes different. Having already known that the United States is ranked fifth in terms of simple metrics of income per capita, and Poland 31st, then using the HDI rating as the criterion for the assessment, they are ranked 15th and 32nd, and according to IHDI – 28th and 27th, respectively[9].

---

7. OECD, Better Live Index (http://www.oecdbetterlifeindex.org/#/00000000000).

8. OECD, Stat (https://stats.oecd.org/Index.aspx?DataSetCode=PDB_LV).

9. NDP, Inequality Adjusted Human Development Index (http://hdr.undp.org/en/content/inequality-adjusted-human-development-index-ihdi).

| Method of economics

The objective of economic activity, to which sustainable development is supposed to lead, stems from the nature of a good economy. In turn, this objective determines the further subject of economic research and its method. A special feature of good economics is its comprehensiveness (Arthur, 2015) because there is always a bundle of conditions, efficient causes, and secondary mechanisms related to the phenomena and processes analyzed and explained. After all, a comprehensive approach is far from universalism, even hostile to "everythingism", but the awareness that things happen as they do because many things happen simultaneously lies at the heart of the research method. By no means does the imperative of economic comprehensiveness signify that one has to touch everything that is close to its subject but anything that is relevant to the shape of a given phenomenon and process cannot be overlooked.

Today, due to the irreversibility of globalization, the global aspect of the broadly understood economic relations is particularly important. The quality and efficiency of economic activity derive from the mutual relations not only between the market and the state, but also between the three fundamental elements of this process: the market, the state, and the world, or else, looking from a slightly different angle: the business, the national economy, and the global economy. Economic research cannot therefore be dissociated from the global aspects of economic activity. They make their presence felt both at the mega-economic level when we study the conditions, course and effects of a trade war, and at the macro-level when we analyze the development of the balance of payments, and at the micro-level when we look at the changes in fuel prices at a petrol station.

The fascination with economics comes from the fact that it intellectually enriches, because it is necessary to constantly reach out to other social sciences – philosophy and anthropology, sociology and psychology, law and political science, history and geography. A good economist must not only be able to count – this is still the science that studies efficient economic activity and one has to be able to compare effects with expenditures – but also to feel. Economics has come out of philosophy and lost a little bit when it has moved too far away from it, getting drawn into mathematics too much, with many economists focusing more on how to count than what to count and why. Hence, in its essence, economics should be treated as humanities, although it is most often placed outside of it, but typically, among social sciences. However, it cannot abandon mathematics and have its head in the clouds of philosophical abstraction. It is a great art to reconcile these two very different domains – the hard one and the soft one. The art of combining various points in time and space, which at first sight seem to be chaotically scattered there. There is a method to the chaos.

However, what economics needs more is not chaos, definitely, but an order and discipline of thought. Here, classical logic is helpful. From a methodological point of view, deduction is as useful as inductive reasoning. Logical induction, i.e. the formulation of theoretical generalizations based on the observation of phenomena and processes and based on accumulated experience, is particularly recommended. The problem is that, unlike in other branches of science, such as physics and chemistry, the chance for economists to carry out experiments, especially on a macro- and mega-scale, is highly limited, if not impossible at all. History provides us with experience, not laboratories.

Deduction, which is a type of logical reasoning the aim of which is to come to a specific conclusion based on an assumed set of premises, offers plenty of opportunities but also poses great risks. Economists almost constantly make assumptions, with this famous "let us suppose that...". The problem is that often the assumptions made are too abstract, detached from reality, illusory, questionable, biased, or simply wrong.

A very dangerous logical fallacy from an intellectual point of view – so often made in social sciences and, in particular, in economics – is the claim: *post hoc ergo propter hoc*, meaning "after this, therefore because of this". The economic growth in the USA that happened between 2016 and 2019 is attributed by President Trump to the decisions behind what others have called "Trumponomics", although it happened largely due to other factors, especially the positive inertia of the previous period, bottom-up technological progress, the good external situation, and favorable energy prices. In Europe, for example, *post hoc ergo propter hoc* thinking is evident when opponents of the introduction of the common currency of the European Union, euro, in countries such as Poland or Sweden, the Czech Republic or Hungary, use the false argument that it increases inflation. The fact is that Lithuania and Slovakia did experience a slight acceleration in the rate of price increases after joining the eurozone, but not for this reason. This was due to the simultaneous operation of cost-push inflation mechanisms, mainly driven by rising labor costs and energy prices.

The biggest logical fallacy of the *post hoc ergo propter hoc* type is the thesis spread by the neoliberal thought that the accumulation of income and wealth inequalities is caused by objective factors, namely out-of-control globalization and the nature of technological progress. That is not true. Globalization itself contributes to a greater increase in income than it would occur in the absence of it. Rising inequalities are not a by-product of globalization and technological progress, but are the result of non-inclusive institutions and bad government policies consciously pursued in a flawed socio-economic and political system (Atkinson, 2018; Milanovic, 2016; Klein and Pettis, 2020). The enrichment of a few at the expense of the many – and this is what neoliberalism is all about[10]– requires specific policies and deregulation of the economy that weakens the supervisory role of the state (Harvey, 2005: Kolodko, 2011). This is accompanied by certain changes in the fiscal system – in taxation, public transfers, and expenditures – which result in capturing of the lion's share of national income growth by the wealthiest sections of the society (Milanovic, 2011; Saez and Zucman, 2019; Tanzi, 2018). Of course, when the national income falls, they are pushing the burden of the recession onto the poorer sections of the population. It is also not the wave of the great technological progress

---

10. Some authors, while agreeing with the observation that a few have become rich at the expense of the many, claim that this is not so much the result of the essence of neoliberalism as it is its effect. Maybe even a side-effect; it was meant well, but it just happened. Well, no. This was the intention, this is how it was supposed to be, and this is how it turned out.

that contributes to unacceptable inequalities. Where such inequalities are really caused by this factor – mainly as a result of the above-average growth rate in the incomes of high-tech professionals, inventors, managers, and skilled workers – they are socially tolerable. It was not without reason that Wall Street was occupied, and not Silicon Valley.

The good economy has to reach out widely to comparative studies. Whoever compares more, knows more. It is as intellectually prolific as it is a complicated method because the question arises as to what to compare with what? This is always linked to the purpose of the research. It is easier to compare what it is and how it is happening here, in our place, with what is happening somewhere else; for example, the competitiveness of the economies of Thailand and Malaysia, or the standard of living in Finland and Romania, or the impact of the interest rate on inflation in Egypt and Turkey. It is also not difficult to consider the current state of affairs against the back-ground of the past; of course, as long as the hypocrisy of historical policy does not meddle with it, which happens from Poland and Russia to Australia and Japan. By contrast, it is more problematic to compare the facts with what could have happened in the other option if the analysis is retrospective (counterfactual history, or what if?), and the hardest thing to do is compare what will happen as a result of suggested or taken actions with what could have happened in the future if some other option had been chosen. This last field of economic comparative studies is fundamental for the rational behavior.

One needs to know how to compare. Comparisons are supposed to make thoughts more comprehensive, provoke additional questions, which first complicate the studied matter, to later explain it better. When one compares different points, even distant in time and space, new dilemmas emerge, additional doubts appear, and inspiring reflections arise. The study does not stop at the surface of the phenomena, but looks further, reaches deeper, senses better. The results of some comparisons – sometimes surprising or even shocking – lead to subsequent ones that bring us closer to drawing right conclusions and formulating correct theoretical concepts. For example, if life satisfaction comparisons suggest that, in this respect, Poland ranks between Trinidad and Tobago and Colombia in 43rd place, and Singapore in 31st place, between Italy and Brazil[11], this cannot go unchallenged, especially for someone who knows all these sites from first-hand experience. This makes us take a closer look at the assumptions in the construction of the rankings, think about the selection of observation fields, critically verify the methods of estimating the values of

11. According to the ranking of "The World Happiness Report 2020" (https://happiness-report.s3.amazonaws.com/2020/WHR20.pdf).

parameters and their weighting. If, as a result of such a thought process, these results are only rejected, without suggesting anything better in exchange, then it is still a creative process, because more questions are already known and, perhaps, more answers.

For the research methods of economics, it should also not be so indifferent that it has grown out of general social interests typical of moral philosophy. This is how Adam Smith created it, publishing *The Theory of Moral Sentiments* in 1759. Even earlier, analogies were sought between economic reality and the functioning of living organisms. In the economy that economics deals with, as in the human body, examined by doctors, there are sometimes hopeless cases where nothing can be done. This makes prevention all the more important in medicine, and in economics, too, it is of paramount importance to recognize that the problem is growing in advance and to prevent it from escalating. A man passes away, but society and humankind persist. So are the diseases that affect them. That is why practical economics is needed so much. What is needed is pragmatism. New pragmatism.

New pragmatism is an outline of a theoretical concept within the postulative trend of economic science based on the desire for a good economy corresponding to the conditions of contemporaneity[12]. It is an original, heterodox profile of the economic theory created as an answer to the challenges of civilization and the transformations of economic systems. A key element of the necessary economic paradigm shift is to move away from the diktat of profit maximization and quantitative production growth as the objective of economic activity and to redefine it, taking into account the imperative of subordinating short-term private capital interests to long-term public interests. An important principle governing the economy of the future should be moderation, i.e. the conscious adjustment of the size of human, material, and financial flows and resources to the requirement of a long-term harmony.

Under new pragmatism, economics is treated as a science, which is:

> 1. *Heterodox* – the course of thought is free from dogma and the compulsion to fit within the framework of orthodox economic doctrines.

---

12. The term "new pragmatism" is used here without any relation to the philosophical current, also known as "new pragmatism" (Gunn, 1992), which was formed in the late 19th century. It was introduced (Kolodko, 2011) not as something contrary to the "old pragmatism", but by using the phrase "new" in a sense of "different", different from what it was previously.

2. *Descriptive* – the analysis and description of the state of affairs constitute a foundation of the diagnosis and a starting point for further considerations.

3. *Explanatory* – the interpretation of the observed phenomena and processes makes it easier to understand why they manifest themselves and occur as they do and not otherwise.

4. *Evaluative* – the evaluation of alternative *ex post* situations and expected *ex ante* results forces us to seek answers to the question of whether it could have been better and whether it can be better in the future.

5. *Normative* – postulating directions and methods of change for the better following the statement concerning what and why seems to be better.

6. *Comprehensive* – the observation of the whole of economic relations in the broadest sense is against reductionism and an attempt to build comprehensive theories from fragmented research results.

7. *Eclectic* – connects the lines of the analysis and synthesis of various economic schools: from behavioral economics through neo-Keynesian economics and institutional economics to development economics and political economics, as well as microeconomics with macroeconomics and global economics.

8. *Contextual* – the analyses and syntheses are not carried out detached from reality, in "pure" economic models but with reference to specific, dynamic,

and variable complex circumstances, conditions, constraints, and opportunities.

9. *Multidisciplinary* – the analysis of the economic reality takes into account the findings and methods of other social sciences disciplines.

10. *Comparative* – comparing in time and space of the economic, cultural, political, geographical, and environmental reality is treated as a basic research method. The scientific process largely consists of comparing and drawing conclusions from this exercise.

The methodological phenomenon of the economic science is manifested in the fact that it is a cognitive process different from that of other social sciences. Therefore, first of all, it comes down to:

1. *describing* (descriptive analysis), then
2. *comparing* (comparative analysis) and
3. *evaluating* (axiological analysis) and, consequently
4. *recommending* (normative analysis)

Descriptively, new pragmatism explains the historical development process, highlighting not only the importance of the individual drivers but also their co-occurrence (coincidence). Normatively, new pragmatism indicates prosperity in its broadest sense as an objective of the economic activity process. The pursuit of it requires:

1. *Economically sustainable development*, that is concerning commodity and capital markets and

investment and finance markets, as well as the workforce.

2. *Socially sustainable development*, that is concerning the distribution of income accepted by the population which is both fair and conducive to the accumulation of capital, and adequate access to public services.

3. *Environmentally and spatially sustainable development*, that is concerning maintaining appropriate relations between human business activity and nature, both on an ongoing basis and in a forward-looking manner. The spatial aspect is also important, without proper consideration of which there is no natural, architectural and urban harmony.

The normative (postulative) current of new pragmatism is the applied economics. It is not a real economic policy at the macro-level and also not a practical management at the micro-level, but theoretical knowledge of how to implement a good economic policy effectively and how to manage a company efficiently. New pragmatism somewhat links the economic theory with the proposals for the economic practice, both at a company and household level, as well as at the state and national economy level. In this context, it is also worth repeating after the eminent British economist, Joan Robinson, that an economist's answer is a question to a politician.

James Kenneth Galbraith (2019a) sees new pragmatism in the continuation of the economic thought of his eminent father, John Kenneth Galbraith (1958). He delivered one of his lectures under the title *Old and New Pragmatism: Challenges and Opportunities for Economics* (Galbraith, 2019b), and in an interview with Polish daily *Rzeczpospolita*, he states: "I was talking about pragmatism in economics. This is the approach that my father, John Kenneth Galbraith, promoted, and which is continued by Prof. Grzegorz Kolodko. Contemporary economics is a much ideologized, abstract field of science, full of theoretical concepts, which are difficult to relate to reality not only for a layman. Nothing like perfect competition or overall balance really exists. I believe that an economist should be useful above all." (Galbraith, 2019c)

New pragmatism is useful and helpful, because it is an economic idea that responds to the challenges of the present, and does not escape from them. It is useful because it is heterodox in nature and is not stuck in the corset of the remnants of the orthodox economy that are breaking away from life. Finally, it is helpful because, based on comprehensive and comparative research, it proposes inclusive institutions and state regulations concerning the private sector in such a way that the economic activity would serve individual and collective needs of the population best.

| Conclusions

Despite the coincidence of many megatrends that influence the way economic activity is conducted, in the foreseeable future it will not change so much that one would speak of a reality completely different than before. The surrounding realities will be the result of a dialectic of continuity and change, and although the scale of technological, cultural, demographic, social, and political changes is indeed enormous, taking also into account the aftermath of the Covid-19 pandemic, the continuity will prevail. In no way does this mean that the previous economic thought can and should dominate. It needs to be significantly rebuilt. Economics must be more innovative and future-oriented, rather than orthodox and generalizing conclusions from observations of the past. Thus, economics faces a number of challenges brought about by the social relations it analyses and describes, in particular the need to redefine the objective of economic activity.

A breakthrough similar to that of the Keynesian revolution that followed the crisis of 1929-1933 is not to be expected. What can be expected are gradual changes in the methods of research and expansion of the exploration fields of economic sciences towards interdisciplinary approaches. There will be no single dominant economic trend, but various schools of thought will exist side by side. Economics will become more eclectic and contextual, using comparative studies as one of the main research tools more than before. Several new currents of economic thought have already emerged against this background, including new pragmatism emphasizing the imperative of moderation in economic activity and the feedback loops between the triple – economically, socially, and ecologically – balanced development.

Part II

The Great Chinese Transformation:
from the Third to the First World

Three worlds in one

In the era of irreversible globalization, the worldwide economic and political rules of play must take account of the growing importance of China. Rather than fight the country, one should pragmatically cooperate on solving the mounting global problems. Contemporarily, both China should adapt to the external world and the world itself should adapt to China. There is no possibility of imposing on it a model developed elsewhere, especially that these days liberal democracy is experiencing a systemic crisis in many countries. Neither is there a chance to impose the Chinese model on others, though it seems tempting to many a country; it is not an exportable "commodity", but its elements may prove useful elsewhere. China is not aiming for global domination; instead, it is consistently integrating with the world to maintain its own development. The only reasonable way forward is thorough observation, mutual learning and pragmatic collaboration based on non-orthodox economic thought. The world is still big enough to fit us all in. Potentially, not necessarily. What we need to make it happen is a proper policy, which, in the future, must also involve its better coordination at a supranational level.

The idea of the so called Third World was never clear. In the decades preceding 1989, it was most often assumed, without going into the intricacies of terminology and definition, that the First World is the highly developed capitalism headed by the United States, the Second World is state socialism with the Soviet Union at the helm, and the Third World is all the rest – most often poor and backward countries, in many cases, especially in Africa – ones still shaking off the legacy of colonialism. One would also often refer to this group of countries as developing countries, though in many cases development was not one of their characteristics. In such a triple division, the Third World was characterized by low output and living standards, and by a large population and a quick growth thereof. Even back then one already had to wonder to which world China belonged. Certainly not to the first one, from which it was separated by an unbridgeable gap, but to the second or third one?

China did not wish to be classified as the "second world" as it would not accept the "with the Soviet Union at the helm" formula, while being unable to put itself at its helm. Maybe in the very beginning of the People's Republic of China's existence, in early 1950s, it had accepted Soviet political predominance but later this changed. Curiously, the Chinese leader Mao Zedong (1893-1976), in the final years of his rule put the USSR in the same group as the USA. In 1974 he said: "In my view, the United States and the Soviet Union belong to the First World. The in-between Japan, Europe and Canada belong to the Second World. The Third World is very populous. Except Japan, Asia belongs to the Third World. So does the whole of Africa and Latin America." (Mao Zedong, 1974)[13]. Of course the "Third World" defined this way should have had China at its helm to be able to stand up to the other two worlds and follow its own, only legitimate way towards a better future.

At that time China was already the world's most populated country, inhabited by 22.5 percent of global population, but it was also one of the poorest countries with a very backward agriculture producing as little as 2.8 percent of the global output. To realize how extreme the poverty was there, it is enough to be aware that, according to today's poverty measure (USD 3.20 per person a day at purchasing power parity, PPP), in the initial years of the PRC more than 99 percent of the society suffered from it! This was truly a country of paupers. Now the poor people represent less than 1 percent[14]. Poverty is a relative term.

---

13. It would be interesting to know where Chairman Mao saw the place of Central and Eastern European countries in his classification.

14. According to the World Bank's estimates, during the four decades of China's market reforms and opening to the world, over 850 million people got out of poverty in China. However, as many as 373 million people are still living on less than USD 5.50 a day over there, that is below the poverty line set for upper-middle income economies, a category to which China belongs (World Bank, 2020a).

Its definitions and scales vary. The ambitious Chinese plan to eliminate poverty altogether in 2020 would mean a situation where the economy and social policy provide everyone with a net annual income above RMB 2300, an equivalent of ca. USD 324 at the market exchange rate, and of ca. USD 684 at purchasing power parity. Unfortunately, the perturbation brought by the Covid-19 outbreak will doubtless delay this historic achievement.

There is a saying I once heard in Africa: if you want to go fast, go alone, if you want to go far, go together. China is showing to all humankind – both the rich and, more importantly, the poor – that one can both go fast and far. In just a lifetime of two generations – between 1979 and 2020, when the population figure has risen by ca. 45 percent, from 970 million to 1.4 billion – China has increased its output measured with gross domestic product, GDP, the unprecedented 40 times. It's hard to believe but these are the facts[15]. Considering the purchasing power and its changes, GDP has grown from ca. USD 690 billion to nearly 27 trillion. According to the same PPP measure, GDP per capita has risen nearly 27 times in this period, exceeding the world average by 6-7 percent.

---

15. At constant prices for 2010, China's real GDP rose from nearly USD 290 billion in 1978 to ca. 11.5 trillion in 2019 according to "World Bank national accounts data, and OECD National Accounts data files"
(https://data.worldbank.org/indicator/NY.GDP.MKTP.KD?locations=CN).

As is always the case with such comparisons, we are dealing with a whole lot of methodological issues as there is more than one way to calculate and more than one comparative measure. According to other estimates, China's GDP per capita has risen from just USD 1600 in 1978 to almost 16,000 in 2019, or exactly ten times. In both cases these are values calculated at constant prices for 2018 but subject to different assumptions and appraisals of changes to the purchasing power, hence the significant differences. The author of those alternative estimates, the Conference Board, in particular believes that the official Chinese data seriously underestimate the historical base or point of reference – income in 1978 (CB, 2020).

It is hard to miss the identical GDP level per capita in the USA in 1978 and in Poland in 2019. If the differences

Table 1: The value and dynamics of GDP of China, USA and Poland, 1978–2019 (PPP)

Total GDP Billion 2018 US$						
Official data				Alternative estimation		
	1978	2019	Quotient 2019/1978	1978	2019	Quotient 2019/1987
China	691	26,952	39.0x	1516	21,956	14.5x
USA	7252	20,993	2.9x	-	-	-
Poland	476	1257	2.6x	-	-	-
Per capita GDP 2018 US$						
China	723	19,387	26.8x	1586	15,973	10.1x
USA	32,574	63,126	1.9x	-	-	-
Poland	13,631	32,775	2.4x	-	-	-

Sources: The Conference Board Total Economy Database (CB, 2020) and own calculations.

in the level of development and living standards only boiled down to that, the countries would not be so far apart. After all, what are four decades on the long path of history?

According to the World Bank's classification, developed high income countries are economies with a Gross National Income (GNI) per capita of USD 12,375. This time it's not GDP but GNI, though the two categories are not far apart. For China GNI is lower than GDP by around 6 percent and in 2019-2020 it could be estimated at ca. USD 10,200. Hence, the high income country status is not far away; all it takes to reach it is a ca. 20 percent growth. Once the shock related to the Covid-19 pandemic has been successfully dealt with, this should take three, maybe four years[16]. And that is how, in merely half a century, between 1974 – when Mao rightly saw China in the Third World – and 2024, the country will have moved its economy to the First World. Although … Although it is far more complicated, because quantity is not all that counts. Sometimes it even counts less than quality.

---

[16]. This may happen but does not have to. Some think that the post-pandemic world will prove much worse for China, which will slow down its growth and greatly lengthen its path to catching up with richer economies. According to those opinions, the West may isolate itself more, blocking the influx of Chinese capital, slow down the knowledge- and technology-sharing and introduce further trade restrictions. The decline in mutual trust will also affect the West-East relations.

Long, long time ago…

The Chinese path to the "First World" has a rich and complex history. On a short timeline, it is usually traced back to its opening to globalization and the attendant liberal economic reforms of Mao's successor, Deng Xiaoping (1904-1997). His famous quip "It doesn't matter if a cat is black or white, as long as it catches mice" is truly the quintessence of pragmatism that has informed Chinese market reforms of the past four decades.

A yet shorter timeline starts with the change of narrative during the rule of Xi Jinping, the Party's current leader since the end of 2012, and the President of the PRC since the spring of 2013. Xi said: "The path, the theory, the system, and the culture of socialism with Chinese characteristics have kept developing, blazing a new trail for other developing countries and nations to achieve modernization. It offers a new option for other countries and nations who want to speed up their development while preserving independence; and it offers Chinese wisdom and a Chinese approach to solving the problems facing mankind." (China Daily, 2017, p. 8)

On a very long timeline of the past, the situation varied; at times China was closer to more developed countries and economies, occasionally even leading the world, some other times the distance was growing and sometimes it was even lagging far behind. Leaving aside ancient times – the highly developed civilization of the Confucius era (551-479 BCE) – these days there are frequent mentions of the admiral of great sea voyages Zheng He (1371-1433), who reached Arabia and eastern coasts of Africa 600 years ago.

In the late 16th and early 17th century some of the illustrious European minds had high regard for Chinese achievements, treating them as a sign of higher level of development. Gottfried Leibniz, German philosopher and mathematician believed that in the field of exact science the West was at the leading edge, while the Chinese surpassed Europeans in "practical philosophy", in the way it organized the society where "laws are beautifully directed towards the greatest tranquillity and order" (Obbema, 2015). Leibniz, learning about China from Catholic missionaries returning from there, and living in a Germany ravaged by the Thirty Years' War (1618-1648), wished Chinese missionaries would arrive in Europe and dreamt of a new global culture combining the best of China and Europe. Nearly 400 years have passed; missionaries – now civilian rather than Jesuit ones – imbued with all kind of ideas travel both ways with unprecedented frequency, and yet this longed-for global culture is still far ahead …

A century and a half later, Voltaire (1694-1778), a great philosopher and writer of *The Enlightenment*, wrote of China with esteem. He was certainly inclined to do so by the background of crisis and chaos prevailing in the pre-revolutionary France. When in 1764 he observed: "Their empire is the best that the world has ever seen" (*op. cit.*, p. 18), he presumably met with similarly critical reactions to those experienced by today's apologists of the complex Chinese reality. Voltaire even created poems about the Qianlong Emperor (1711-1799), whom he perceived as a Platonic philosopher-king.

Hard as it is to believe, two hundred years ago China produced ca. 32 percent of the global output. It will be easier to understand, however, when we realize that back then the country was inhabited by more people than now in relative terms; ca. 38 percent of the entire world's population. There were more than three times as much of Chinese people as Europeans; 381 and 122 million respectively. Then there came a period of slowdown and regression. While first Europe, and then North America were gathering momentum as a result of subsequent industrial revolutions, China – not without help from some empires of Western Europe – descended into stagnation. In the late 19th and early 20th century it was a semi-colonized economy. That "century of national humiliation" is often recalled today. It is known to all primary school pupils, making them even prouder of their homeland's contemporary achievements and avid for something worthy of being the Chinese Dream of 21st century.

History never repeats itself to the letter, but sometimes the contemporaries cannot help but be reminded of the past. The Chinese were once already the object of fear, or to be more exact, that of scaremongering, amid a surge of xenophobia. The end of 19th century in both North America and Europe went down in history as the inglorious time of "Yellow Peril". It was essentially an anti-Asian racism where fear of migrants from the region was deliberately instilled in the local population, and disgraceful racist practices were resorted to, at times, on the grounds of the American and European civilization… In the USA in 1882 the Chinese Exclusion Act was enacted, which was repealed in 1943, and the Senate apologized for it only in 2011 (sic!). Had it not done it back then, this certainly would not have happened now, with a Republican majority. Whereas in Europe in the late 19th century the German Kaiser Wilhelm II would fuel the hatred towards the Chinese with the threatening vision of their invading hordes. It was to that end that he sent to his distant cousin, the tsar of Russia Alexander III, a drawing depicting a Chinese dragon trampling over the Christian Europe. The multiple copies of the image had a vast success as contemporarily do some chauvinistic and racist memes.

The inability to go with the creative and pro-development flow of industrial revolutions in the 19th century, as well as the social and military shocks of the first half of the 20th century caused China to be incapable, for a couple of generations, of overcoming a systemic – economic and political – collapse. China's GDP in mid-20th century, when the People's Republic of China was founded, with the Communist Party of China at its helm, represented no more than a meagre 2 percent of the global output. This fall – as a fall it was – in the form of a drastic downward slide in just 130 years from a situation where the country produced one third of the global output to producing merely its one-fiftieth, coupled with the immense population it affected, was an unprecedented process.

From ever more to ever better

Now, at purchasing power parity, China's GDP is back to ca. 20 percent of the world's output. Over time, the figure will keep growing; one day reaching again over 30 percent, like two centuries ago. This has its obvious determinants and less obvious implications. It is the Chinese political and economic system that has enabled such progress, especially in the period of reform and opening-up post-1978 (Lin, 2012a; *Economy*, 2018). However, it comes at a huge cost and yields negative consequences the GDP value alone fails to show. Particularly acute are the ecological costs in the form of environmental devastation and the immense scale of income inequalities. These two areas – in addition to the need for economic equilibrium especially with respect to finance and trade – represent the greatest challenges faced by the economic policy in the coming decades. Improving the environmental situation and reducing income and wealth differences are issues of more importance than constantly maximizing the rate of the traditionally defined economic growth.

Naturally, the latter cannot be disregarded. After all, it is the value of goods produced and services supplied that provides the material foundations of life and determines the wellbeing. Moreover, maintaining a relative balance on the labour market requires, as can be estimated, at least a 5 percent GDP growth rate. The economy needs to absorb each year over a dozen million employees migrating to industries and services located in urban areas. This is one of the conditions for keeping social peace, much more important than catching up with and outpacing others. After all, the reason why China has the policy of fast economic growth in place is not to be able to outdo Japan and the USA in terms of output, but to better satisfy the needs of its numerous population.

China has picked up speed. Its economic dynamic greatly exceeds that of highly developed countries, constantly reducing the gap[17]. What also matters in the context of geopolitics is that in the second decade of the 21st century India's economy is growing almost just as fast. In the previous 30 years it was not the case, which is of significance for discussions comparing different political and economic models; in 1980-2009 India's total GDP rose ca. 7.2-fold, and in China, as much as ca. 26.7-

---

17. It is worth comparing, subject to all relevant methodological reservations, the economic dynamic of China with the country of the most successful post-socialist transition, Poland (Piatkowski, 2018; Kolodko, 2020b). Well, Poland's GDP approximately tripled in the three decades between 1990 and 2019, whereas that of China increased as much as 15 times. Per capita, for Poland this is still more or less three times as much, because the population has slightly decreased, while for China, as we know, the real income per capita has grown approximately 12 times.

fold. In that time, India, which until 1992 had a higher income per capita, was left far behind by China. In turn, while total GDP in China in the decade of 2010-2019 slightly more than doubled, in India it almost doubled. Consequently, now a Chinese person's average income is nearly two and a half times as high as that of an Indian person.

Figure 1: The GDP of China and the Big-5 in 2019
Index numbers (2009 = 100)

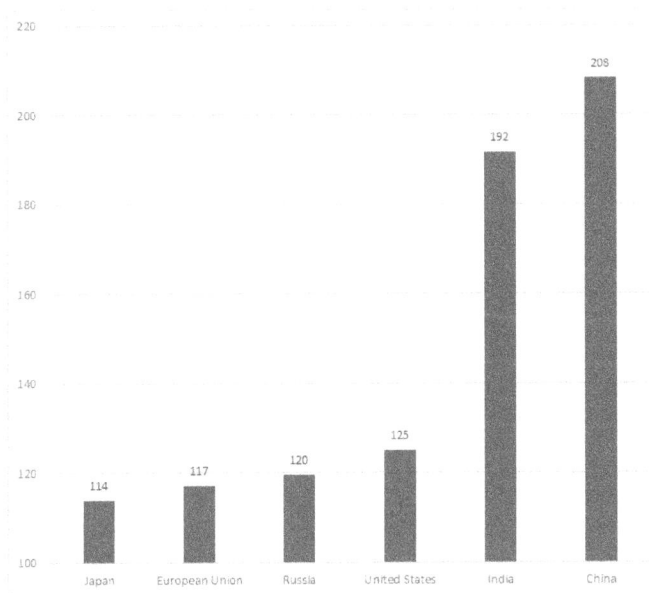

Sources: Own calculations based on the data of WEO (2019).

Though we are already living in a beyond-GDP reality (Kolodko, 2014a; Stiglitz, Fitoussi and Durand, 2018; Koźmiński, Noga, Piotrowska and Zagórski, 2020), let us dwell a while longer on the GDP analysis. It is important because also in this field a lot will change due to the confusion caused by the Covid-19 pandemic. As a matter of fact, according to the estimates of the International Monetary Fund, economic growth is to still continue in 2020 in those former Third World's two largest economies, though on a much lesser scale as a result of the lockdown of part of the economy, intended to prevent the spreading of the contagion, and the disruption of the transnational supply and production chains (Kolodko, 2020c). In its World Economic Outlook for spring IMF forecasted for China and India a GDP growth of 1.2 and 1.9 percent, respectively, in 2020 and an exponential growth of 9.2 and 7.4 percent in 2021 (WEO, 2020)[18]. For highly developed countries a major downturn in output was expected.

Table 2: Forecasts of recession and growth in 2020-2021 (fall/growth of GDP, %)

Country	2020	2021	2021 (2019 = 100)
China	1.2	9.2	110.5
India	1.9	7.4	109.4
Japan	−5.2	3.0	97.6
Russia	−5.5	3.5	97.8
USA	−5.9	4.7	98.5
World	−3.0	5.8	102.6

Sources: WEO (2020).

---

18. At the same time, the European Commission forecasted China's GDP growth in 2020-2021 at 1.0 and 7.8%. (EU 2020).

Should such scenarios materialize, China's GDP at PPP will increase from ca. 128 percent of the US level in 2019 to ca. 144 percent in 2021 or – reversing the perspective – the US income will decrease from 78 to 70 percent of that of China. This is indisputably not the effect desired by the President of the USA Donald Trump, whose policy is intentionally designed to relatively weaken the Chinese economy and "Make America Great Again!" in this context. Therefore, the scale of shifts taking place on the global scene is gigantic. Let me just point out that the China's national income estimated this way is only counterbalanced by the sum total of income of the United States, Japan and Russia.

Figure 2: China versus Big-4
GDP of selected countries in percent of China's GDP (in PPP)

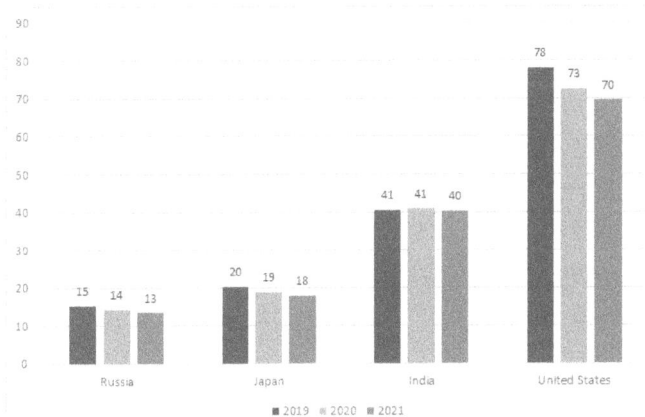

Russia: 15, 14, 13
Japan: 20, 19, 18
India: 41, 41, 40
United States: 78, 73, 70

■ 2019 ▦ 2020 ■ 2021

Sources: WEO (2020).

China's total national income (PPP-weighted GDP) is more than one-fourth higher than that of the USA, whereas at the current exchange rate it is still much, nearly one-third, lower. In 2019 these figures stood at ca. USD 21 trillion and 14.4 trillion. A better and more informative category is income at purchasing power parity as this figure tells us how much it is actually worth, or, more precisely, what comparable value of goods and services it can be converted into, considering the international price differences. If we were to stick in our analyses to income calculated at the market exchange rate, adopting the simplifying assumption that these countries will maintain post-2020 the average GDP growth rate at the level achieved in the year preceding the Covid-19 pandemic, meaning 2.3 and 6.1percent, respectively, then China's GDP, reaching USD 26 trillion (at constant prices for 2019), will exceed the USA's level in 2030.

What also, and sometimes especially, matters in the global economic cooperation and rivalry for political supremacy is how China's output impacts other countries. It was not until 1995 that China made it to the very end of the list of top fifteen global exporters and, just after eighteen years, in 2013, it took the lead which it will continue to hold in the foreseeable future[19]. China's total

---

19. With the incredible frictions caused by the Covid-19 pandemic and the often chaotic economic policy reactions, it is rather a question of unforeseeable future…

Table 3: Top ten countries of Chinese exports, 2019

	bln USD	%
United States	418.6	16.8
Hong Kong, China	279.6	11.2
Japan	143.2	5.7
South Korea	111.0	4.4
Vietnam	98.0	3.9
Germany	79.7	3.2
India	74.9	3.0
Netherlands	73.9	3.0
United Kingdom	62.3	2.5
Taiwan, China	55.1	2.2

Sources: International Trade Centre based on General Customs
Administration of China Statistics (Trade Map 2020) and own calculations.

international trade amounted to USD 4.6 trillion in 2019, with exports up by 0.5 percent and imports down by 2.8 percent compared to the preceding year.

Let us also note that the relatively very high exports to Hong Kong are nearly entirely re-exported by the same. So the actual exportation of goods to respective foreign markets is higher than revealed by the data quoted here.

In the last year before the pandemic that shook the world economy, including the international trade, China had a positive balance of USD 421.5 billion, higher than in the preceding year, despite the sanctions resulting from the trade war waged by the USA. China remains the USA's largest trade partner as, regardless of the protectionist restrictions imposed by President Trump's administration, it is the recipient of goods worth over half a trillion dollars, that is ca. one fifth of total US exports.

Another thing that matters in the global rivalry is the state's financial reserves, in which China, again, with foreign currency reserves worth the equivalent of ca. USD 3.1 trillion, ranks First Worldwide[20]. These reserves were ca. USD 750 billion higher in 2014, but in the following five years they were sensibly used by financial policy to stabilize the economy and stimulate the output growth. It is worth pointing out here that Beijing holds a third of reserves in US securities, binding these two economies even further. Two thirds are distributed among other reserve currencies, euro having the greatest share, followed by yen, Hong Kong dollar[21], British pound sterling, Korean won, Australian and Canadian dollars, and Swiss franc. Approximately USD 100 billion is held in gold.

On the other hand, only ca. 2 percent of the global currency reserves are held in the Chinese currency. It can be estimated that other countries' central banks have accumulated in RMB no more than the equivalent

---

20. It is also worth noting that both Hong Kong and Taiwan, China have reserves that in both cases greatly exceed USD 400 billion. Hence, looking at the whole China, its currency reserves go up to ca. USD 4 trillion.

21. Hong Kong dollar, HKD, is *de facto* pegged to the US dollar under the currency board regime, so from the macroeconomic perspective both currencies can be treated similarly.

of a quarter of a trillion of dollars. That is the current status but it will change and RMB's share of global currency reserves will systematically, though slowly, rise. Undoubtedly, at first at the expense of US dollar, which will also have its political implications. Furthermore, China, provoked by the US hostility and aggressive trade policy that hinders economic development, is consistently setting up a parallel financial system, which will help go around USD-based payment mechanisms (Economist, 2020a). Currently, the way the international financial clearing system works means that a vast number of international trade transactions cannot be concluded bypassing USD. This enables the USA to impose severe sanctions on others or blackmail them with a threat of sanctions, which is being experienced by Iran these days and which also threatens to befall its trade partners.

Sometimes hostile emotions virtually lead to loss of reason. This is what can be said of prominent representatives of the US political establishment formulating accusations against China and demanding financial compensation for the losses sustained by the US economy as a result of the Covid-19 pandemic. The media have reported on the fantastic idea popularized by sources within the administration that the White House is thinking of cancelling part of USD 1.1 trillion debt to China to 'punish' the country for the pandemic." (Economist, 2020b). "Congressional Republicans such as Sen. Lindsey O. Graham (S.C.) have increasingly demanded the United States 'make China pay big time' over the damage." (Stein et.al. 2020). Senator Marsha Blackburn went even further, reaching the absurd, as she "floated waiving interest payments to China for any holdings of US debt, 'because they have cost our economy already $6 trillion and we could end up being an additional $5 trillion hit.'" (ibidem). Such public declarations by major-league politicians are the grist to the mill of xenophobia as if there was not enough of it already. During the electoral campaign, striving for re-election of President Trump, his henchmen are paying for media ads insinuating that "China is killing our jobs and now, killing our people." (Stein et.al., op. cit.). Chinese state-owned media were quick to respond, fanning the nationalist emotions with invectives against Mike Pompeo, the US Secretary of State, calling him "evil", "insane" and a "common enemy of mankind" (ibidem). A fascinating though often nasty clash between geoeconomics and geopolitics is underway. Both these mega-processes are interconnected, but – assuming that we manage to avoid the ruinous hot war, which assumption I consistently make – in the world of tomorrow, economic processes will be undoubtedly of crucial importance. Power relations will be determined by how these unfold rather than by subjective desires and ambitions of politicians for whom power and influence are everything, and solving social and economic problems only serves as an instrument of their dominance. From this standpoint, China's relative position in the global arena will continue to grow stronger for many years to come as its economy will grow in both absolute and relative terms, though no longer at the rate it did until recently.

Population and human capital

The time of quantity will never end, but now the time has come for the next generation quality. Today, and even more so in the future, economic successes will depend less and less on the possession of natural resources, and tangible and financial assets, and increasingly on human capital. Since the dawn of time, economy has relied on knowledge, but never has so much depended on knowledge resources as it does now. It is knowledge and the skills in leveraging it in production and exchange processes that will determine which economy is at the leading edge. The competitiveness of economies increasingly depends on knowledge, which China is fully aware of. Accordingly, the country invests in knowledge and technological progress ever more time and funds.

Chinese universities are working their way up global ranking lists, though they are far from the top positions. Those are occupied nearly entirely by US and British schools (only one continental European university is among top ten: Swiss Federal Institute of Technology in Zurich) with MIT, Stanford and Harvard on the podium, but Tsinghua University already ranks 16th, and Peking University, 22nd (QS, 2020). In top engineering school rankings, Tsinghua is already right after MIT and experts say it is a matter of years before it becomes a world leader.

The results of this cannot yet be seen, for example, in Forbes list showcasing the most valuable brands, where the remote 97th place went to the only Chinese company on the list, indeed the most known and significant on the global, not only economic, scene—Huawei (Forbes, 2020). It wedged in between Danish Lego blocks and US John Deere tractors. Meanwhile, in a much more important ranking, having specific implications for decisions on investments and purchase orders, namely in the Global Competitiveness Index compiled by the World Economic Forum, China ranks 28th, after Malaysia and Iceland and before Qatar and Italy (WEF, 2019). The list starts with Singapore, the USA and Hong Kong, China. Interestingly, in terms of competitiveness, China is ahead of all other BRICS countries – Brazil, Russia, Indonesia and South Africa – and most European Union countries[22].

What will be pivotal for the future is to what extent and how quickly changes will take place as regards satisfaction of the changing needs of the population. The same is ever increasing in countries working their way up

---

22. Specifically, in WEF competitiveness ranking, China ranks higher than Italy, Estonia, Czech Republic, Portugal, Slovenia, Poland, Malta, Lithuania, Latvia, Slovakia, Cyprus, Hungary, Bulgaria, Romania, Greece and Croatia, whose 63th place puts it between the Philippines and Costa Rica (WEF, 2019).

and ever smaller in rich countries which, with exceptions, welcome immigrants. In China, the population will soon cease to grow though it will continue to age.

Table 4: Population growth forecasts, 2020-2060

Year	2020	2060	Growth / Fall
Country			in per cent
China	1439	1333	-7,4
India	1380	1651	19,6
USA	331	391	18,1
Russia	146	133	-8,9
Japan	126	98	-22,2
World	7795	10151	30,2

Sources: UN 2019.

According to UN projections, China's population will start to decline after 2030. Meanwhile, such a turning point will happen for India a generation later, after 2060. It is of significance in this context that India – unlike China and other countries with a quickly ageing population – can leverage its demographic dividend in the form of relatively young population, which is a contributing factor for a dynamic economy. While median age in the former country is around 28 years, in the latter, it is over 37 (the global average being 30 years). Hence, in this respect, China's situation is already unfavourable and it will continue to deteriorate.

The society's condition and the wellbeing of the people, especially the financial circumstances of their households and the assessment of individual economic situation are not determined by the economy size nor by the nation's population. That "we are the largest country" or "we are more numerous than you" counts for something – more in political than in psychological terms – but welfare and the subjective sense thereof is not improving much in China just due to the fact that the Chinese are still the most numerous in the world and that they produce the most at PPP. Likewise, the fact that, say, Indonesians are seven times as numerous as Poles and that in total they produce almost three times as much is little cause for rejoicing for the former if their country's GDP per capita represents only 42 percent of the same category in the latter, where, for this reason, among others, the average lifespan is nearly five years longer. In China, one lives, on average, only two years shorter than in the USA (77 compared to 79 years), enjoying an average income that is rising very fast but still represents only 30 percent of the American income, which stood at USD 64,700 per capita in 2019. These are the reasons why one needs to draw on more adequate information than the simple measure of income per capita. Categories describing the human capital level are highly useful from this perspective.

**Table 5: Human Development and Inequality Adjusted Human
Development Indices**

Country	HDI rank	HDI	IHDI	Overall loss (%)	Difference from HDI rank
Norway	1	0.954	0.889	6.8	0
USA	15	0.920	0.797	13.4	-13
Japan	19	0.915	0.882	3.6	15
Russia	49	0.824	0.743	9.9	1
China	85	0.758	0.636	16.1	4
India	129	0.647	0.477	26.3	1
World	-	0.731	0.584	20.2	-

Note: Overall loss: Percentage difference between the IHDI value and the HDI value.
Sources: UNDP (2019), p. 308-311.

In terms of HDI, the United States ranks 15th, between New Zealand and the United Kingdom, and Belgium and Japan, and China, 85th, between North Macedonia and Peru, and Ecuador and Azerbaijan. Norway tops the list (HDI of 0.954), and Niger is at the bottom (HDI of 0.377). Taking account of income distribution inequalities – very high both in the USA and China, with Gini index of 41.5 and 38.6 respectively – the USA goes down 13 spots, to the 28th place, and China moves up by 4, to the 81st place, so the distance between them is slightly shorter than in income differences.

Another thing that matters is the dynamic of change and the shifts on the world map reflecting differences in the level and quality of human capital. In a period of just three decades, since 1990, the average HDI for the world as a whole has risen from 0.598 to 0.731, whereas in the USA it has gone up from 0.860 to 0.920, and in China from 0.501 to 0.758. Hence, thirty years ago China was below the global average, and now it is already above. While the quality of human capital measured this way has been rising globally by 0.72 percent a year, the pace of its growth in the USA was three times as slow (0.24 percent), and in China, twice as fast (1.48 percent). It goes without saying, of course, that it is easier to work your way up to higher thresholds when you start from a low level. Now it is getting ever more difficult.

| Not only capitalism, also Chinism

Branko Milanović in his interesting book titled
*Capitalism, Alone: The Future of the System That Rules
the World* argues that, though following the fall of the
Soviet-style state socialism (most often referred to in the
literature as communism[23]) the history by no means came
to an end, capitalism triumphantly and universally took
hold over the world (Milanović, 2019). He believes that
the future must follow its path as there is no alternative to
the victorious capitalism. One could reduce the matter to
definitions, but it is much more complicated. Especially
that the author often puts different categories of political
and economic systems under the umbrella term of
"capitalism", distinguishing between its two fundamental
types: meritocratic liberal capitalism headed by the USA

---

23. In the West, already back in the period preceding the turning point of 1989,
the political and economic system dominating the Soviet Union and Central and
Eastern Europe was referred to as communism, while in the part of the world where
the system was spreading, the term "socialism" was used to mean the same. Later,
in the period of systemic transition, also over there one could most often hear the
term "communism" with reference to the period between 1945 and 1989. One
could, therefore, sum up saying that it is a matter of terminology, but it is not true as
significant substantive differences and ideological disputes lie behind the definition
ambiguity (Walicki, 1995; Kolodko, 2000; Nuti, 2018).

and political capitalism headed by China. Therefore, even though the book title speaks of capitalism alone, in the capitalist reality suggested by the author we would deal with more than just one identity.

Perhaps this is the case, but the problem is that rather than two varieties as part of one system, we can see a systemic multiplicity. It is not the same case as that of, say, gorilla and orangutan, two apes belonging to the same family of creatures, but one more similar to that of a monkey and a lemur; very similar on the exterior but different deep down. One can hardly squeeze in such vastly diversified present and future times into one systemic category as there are many of them. We still have several worlds, and the point is to decide which of them deserves to be dubbed the first one, which is the second one and what is going on with the third one, and perhaps with yet a couple more others.

We must agree that there is a need to distinguish between liberal capitalism that evolved in the West over a long historical process, and state capitalism that originated from a shorter historical process in many post-colonial countries – the erstwhile Third World – and some countries of the post-socialist transition. In the first group of state capitalist countries, classical examples would be economies that are as diverse as Saudi Arabia and

Myanmar, in the second group, Russia and Kazakhstan[24].

China differs in terms of quality and it would be too far-fetched to classify it according to that model. This is neither a case of communism, as some would still have it (Fun and Zheng, 2020), nor of capitalism, even one adorned with this adjective or another (Pei, 2016) but that of a different quality. It is a political/social/economic system in its own right which I refer to as Chinism (Kolodko, 2018; 2020a). It is no Beijing Consensus, which some attempted to hail for a time as the antithesis for the neoliberal Washington Consensus (Halper, 2010). Though one can see some analogies between those concepts, there are definitely more significant differences (Lin, 2013). Neither is it a simple period of transition from a centrally-planned economy to a market economy (Lardy 2014).

Chinism, *sui generis*, is a syncretic economic system based on multiple forms of ownership of means of

---

24. Let us leave out of this taxonomy the particular cases that need to be assigned their own pigeonhole. Cuba can be certainly classified as state socialism. A type of its own is DPRK with its unique *Juche* system and ideology (Lankov, 2016). We can be sure that none of those models will have any followers in the future. On the contrary, these countries' greatest opportunity for growth lies in following the hybrid system of China. As a side note, when I crossed the border between DPRK and "socialist" China on the bridge over the Yalu River, I could not resist the impression that I was entering a liberal country where freedom reigns⋯ Everything is relative.

production, with a strong macroeconomic policy and limited government control with respect to micro-economic management. Deregulation is subordinated to maintaining enterprises' activities on the course that is in line with the social and political goals set by the ruling party[25]. Widely used, flexible but generally far-reaching economic interventionism uses both indicative planning addressing the business sphere and command planning with respect to some state-owned enterprises and infrastructure. The country's policy for the government, local authorities and the central bank alike also makes use of classical instruments of market interventionism. The pricing system is essentially decentralized, which, despite not fully hardened budget constraints with respect to public enterprises guarantees maintaining a dynamic money market equilibrium.

At the same time, Chinism has helped eliminate the shortage syndrome and effectively keep price inflation in check. This is a feat none of the former state socialism economies, neither the Soviet Union nor any of CEE economies, was able to accomplish, which was the main reason behind their economic and, consequently, political demise (Kolodko, Rutkowski, 1991; Csaba, 1996).

---

25. The Communist Party of China.

The policy implemented by the state is competent and responsible. At the same time, it is oriented to fulfilling long-term strategic goals, to which medium-term and immediate goals are subordinated.

Chinism does not stand for turning back from the path of market reforms and returning to the omnipotence of the state sector in the economy (Lardy, 2019); this is an overly simplified image of a highly complex reality. The state plays a major role – most of all as a regulator and also as the owner of some means of production – but it does not crowd out nor replaces the market but rather corrects and supports it and creates a synergy with its forces (Huang, 2017). One should not overestimate isolated events nor hastily generalize individual observations, but the fact that in 2008 the prestigious post of Chief Economist and Senior Vice President of Develop-ment Economics at the World Bank was assigned to the eminent Chinese economist, Justin Yifu Lin, was meaningful. This was not an empty gesture directed at China in recognition of the country's achievements from those who in fact decided it – the US authorities in consultation with Japan, the United Kingdom, Germany and France. It was a sign, especially to economically backward countries, that valuable conclusions can be drawn from China's experience in the development policy and it is worth adopting such good practices elsewhere. Lin's term of office, 2008-2012, did not revolutionize Washington's technocratic way of thinking or World Bank's activities, but it undoubtedly contributed to this organization's further departure from neoliberal orthodoxy.

Outside China, the appeal of Chinism is, by definition, limited. Certainly it will not be transposed to countries of liberal capitalism, but, in turn, it can be – and already is – an inspiring offer, or at least an option worth contemplating for many countries of the former Third World, especially in South Asia, Middle East and Africa, and to a lesser extent in South and Central America, and for some post-socialist countries, mainly post-Soviet republics of the Central Asia. Countries of liberal democracy, in the face of the crisis thereof, must look for ways to protect themselves against the wave of new nationalism and the crisis-generating potential of neoliberalism (Galbraith, 2018), but they will surely not follow the Chinese model. This may be done, though to a very diverse extent, by emancipating economies and societies, i.e. those forced by neoliberalism into the category of so called emerging markets. The heart of the matter is that two significant processes overlap in the same time: a huge economic success of Chinism on the one hand, and a structural crisis of liberal capitalism, on the other.

Countries which look for a lighthouse, on this chaotic ocean of global economy, can be more quickly reached by the light from Beijing than from Washington, more clearly from the Pearl River Delta and Guangzhou than from New York and Manhattan. This is also supported by the strong activity of Chinese foreign policy. Beijing has more diplomatic posts scattered around the world than the United States. Its political impact cannot be underestimated but at the same time one should not fear it will outdo the West, including the Anglo-American influence, when it comes to the so called soft power. It is a good thing that in numerous countries more than a hundred Confucius institutes were launched, which promote China and Chinese values. It is no threat, on the contrary; a bit more of us will understand Mandarin, which will also contribute to expanding the international exchange in the sphere of education, science, culture and sports. The next culminating event in the soft power clash will be the 24th Winter Olympic Games in Beijing in 2022, especially after the 2020 Summer Olympics in Tokyo were cancelled.

This external development – irrespective of its strictly economic goals, mainly to export major surpluses in the infrastructure construction sector, develop outlets for ever more competitive industries and get access to deposits of raw materials and inputs – is pursued on a spectacular scale by means of the Belt and Road Initiative (BRI) (Maçães, 2018), often referred to as the new Silk Road. Its principal purpose is not to conquer other countries by making them economically dependent – though this, too, can happen in cases of reckless policy at the recipient country so caution should be exercised – but to maintain an internal economic dynamic. For China, despite the enormous size of the country, this cannot be achieved without having recourse to external factors, without further tapping into globalization for quick growth in domestic production and consumption. Over the last couple of decades nobody has leveraged globalization so well for its own growth as China has. No wonder that it wishes to continue to do so. The Chinese are better positioned to do that as it seems that, unlike people of the West who, on their visits to China tell the locals how the world should be organized, the Chinese, while traveling, look around for solutions that may prove useful also to them. Probably China has learnt more from the West over the last decades than the West has from China, though quite a lot of things could be learnt there, too.

BRI – and the attendant policy instrumentation and system institutileonalization, as exemplified by the relatively easily accessible loans from state-owned Eximbank or the establishing of a multinational investment bank, Asian Infrastructure Investment Bank (AIIB) – warrants a broader perspective. It is not a threat to the West, and not to Western Europe, either, considering the part of BRI known as 16+1, and 17+1[26] since Greece followed in the footsteps of post-socialist CEE economies in 2019[27] and again 16+1 after Lithuania withdrew from it in 2021. Though much hope was pinned on 16+1, its first seven years have proved rather lean.

Elsewhere, the swift inflow of Chinese infrastructure and manufacturing investments, and trade cooperation as well as staff training and healthcare offering may result in additional development. Let us look at a broader picture; the faster this growth bears fruit, the greater will be the benefits reaped directly in the countries to which investments and economic aid are addressed. The lower, too, will be the pressure to migrate from poor countries of Asia and Africa to Europe, and the smaller will be the influx of refugees and economic migrants, the waves of which the Europeans have a tough time handling.

---

26. China has put 17 countries in one basket for obvious geographic—and, to be more precise, geoeconomic and geopolitical reasons—but also taking account of the difference of scale. It would suffice to realize that the sum total of GDPs of those 17 CEE economies represents merely ca. 14 percent of China's GDP (ca. 16 percent at PPP).

27. The 16 CEE countries invited by Beijing in 2012 to join BRI are: Albania, Bosnia and Herzegovina, Bulgaria, Croatia, Czech Republic, Estonia, Hungary, Latvia, Lithuania, Montenegro, North Macedonia, Poland, Romania, Serbia, Slovakia and Slovenia. This group does not include Belarus, Moldova and Ukraine. It does not feature Kosovo, either, whose independence China has not recognized to date and neither have Chinese maps as they still show Kosovo as part of Serbia.

Battle for tomorrow, or the imperative of inclusive globalization

Ironically, it is the coronavirus-induced impossibility to maintain live face-to-face contacts that brings to the fore the strong and unbridled human desire to travel and absorb other cultures, work together in the field of education and scientific research, exchange and sports rivalry. We want to be together, not apart. These factors, not less than the classical links as part of production, supply and sales chains and global trade make globalisation – understood as the integration of capital and goods markets following liberalization – irreversible. It is all the more surprising that the calling into question came from the least expected direction. The opinion-leading liberal weekly *The Economist* comes out with a screaming cover title: Goodbye globalisation advising its readers: "Wave goodbye to the greatest era of globalisation—and worry about what is going to take its place." (*Economist*, 2020c). It can be surmised that its diagnosis is not only due to the pandemic's devastating consequences for liberalization and world economy integration but also that the magazine has understood that the existing form of extractive globalization stands no chance anymore, while it doubts the success of its inclusive version.

It is true that the pandemic – with its psychological and political side effects such as growing xenophobia and mutual hostility – is highlighting the symptoms of protectionism and naïve mercantilism that could already be felt before. The neoliberalism-induced financial and economic crisis of 2008 led to a wave of new nationalism. For neoliberalism, intended to help very few get rich at the expense of the majority, the public enemy was the government as the regulator and income redistribution policy maker, whereas for populism and new nationalism, this role is reserved for globalization. This clash both weakens the capacity – already an impaired one – to focus policymaking on the multinational scale, and is conducive to throwing political, social and economic relations into anarchy.

Adding to the crisis of mishandled economy liberalization – it being improperly deregulated from the point of view of social cohesion and economic equilibrium – is the crisis of liberal democracy (Krastev and Holmes, 2019). There are those who believe that liberalism has already collapsed (Deneen, 2018). This crisis is taking different, sometimes surprising forms – one in the USA following the election of President Donald Trump, another one in Poland ruled by Law and Justice Party; yet another one in Australia with its nationalist government of Prime Minister Scott Morrison, and a different one in Brazil with the populist right-wing President Jair Bolsonaro. In every case it harms the supranational social cohesion and makes it difficult for globalisation to stay on a reasonable course.

This course must be based on the non-orthodox economic thought, of particular importance being new structural economics (Lin, 2012b), economics for the common good (Tirole, 2017) and new pragmatism— a sort of interface between descriptive and prescriptive economics indicating the ways to integrate economic, social and environmental development into an economy of moderation (Kolodko, 2014b; 2021). The belief that, though hard, it is possible to create a good economy, is voiced by economists of various contemporary theoretical schools (Galbraith, 2014; Phelps, 2013; Rodrik, 2015; Stiglitz, 2019a).

China – this greatest beneficiary of globalization – fully grasps that, which is why (though above all, because it has its own interests at heart), it is its great advocate. To save globalization, to make it truly irreversible, it must become inclusive. Letting it continue in its neoliberal variety preferred by interest groups and selfish economic and political lobbies, coinciding with adverse megatrends in natural environment changes, global warming, uncontrollable large migrations and the Covid-19 pandemic, which has led to what I call a Yet Greater Crisis, YGC (Kolodko, 2011; 2020c), is not an option.

Not only an inclusive globalization, but also no globalization whatsoever can be continued without the necessary degree of harmony between the world's two largest economies – that of China and the USA (Kissinger, 2011). When it already seemed that we were on the right track in this respect—especially thanks to the efforts of President Barack Obama and President Xi Jinping, yielding a number of bilateral and multilateral agreements of global implications, as exemplified by the fundamental 2015 Paris Agreement on climate change mitigation – there came President Donald Trump, a sworn enemy of globalization who fails to understand its essence. The hope for development of *pro publico mundiale bono* cooperation and friendly rivalry as part of the so called G-2 – or Chimerica—was replaced with Cold War 2.0. The reason why it is dangerous is that in addition to Donald Trump's extreme Sinophobia, republicans' democratic opponents are not fully devoid of the same. It will take some time before better pragmatism-driven relations can be re-established…

An interesting perspective, one that systematizes the analyses and provides a methodology to facilitate the discussion of China's foreign relations is suggested by Kerry Brown. In his inspiring study *What Does China Want? China's World* he divides China's global surrounding into four zones. The first one is the United States, the second, the rest of Asia (including Russia), the third, the European Union and the fourth, other countries of the world (Brown, 2017). The China-US relations are paramount for the functioning of the global economy and politics; with or without globalization. Another thing of strategic importance is the behaviour of the European Union, which President Trump would like to win over to his side in the US-China face-off. He is failing at that and one should hope that nobody will succeed in turning the EU and China against each other as that would harm them both and the whole global economy alike.

Hard times call for prudence and calm rather than thoughtlessness and overexcitement. Some Western politicians, failing to comprehend the objective imperative of pragmatic co-existence with China, have radically turned their backs to it. This can be felt much stronger in the USA than in the EU. Now, in the face of their own powerlessness, they are losing common sense. While in politics one cannot entirely avoid madmen and fools who need to be restrained and eliminated from public life, some statements by top-echelon politicians and influential government advisors are in the highest degree alarming. These are people we expect expertise and responsibility from, and if they are guided by cynicism, so common in politics, this should be exposed and opposed to in a debate. If they are losing their heads due to their impotence, things start to get out of hand.

When an expert of the stature of Peter Navarro, an economic advisor to whom President Trump lends an ear, says China "inflicted tremendous damage (…) We're up to close to $10 trillion we've had to appropriate to fight this battle (…) A bill has to come due for China (…) it's a question of holding China accountable, the Chinese Communist Party accountable", it is already dangerous. Could it be "Yellow Peril" 2.0? Maybe it would be more legitimate for China to claim from the West, especially from the British, a compensation for giant losses caused knowingly by the intentionally waged Opium Wars in mid-19th century where half-colonized Chinese population was subjected to planned debilitation by being forced to buy poison cultivated by poor peasants in fully-colonized India? Let us just wait for somebody to come up with such a demand... Maybe Central and Eastern Europe will also demand to be paid back for the losses brought on by the Washington-championed "Consensus" at the time of post-socialist transition? And, while we're at it, the countries of Western Africa may demand retribution for the irreparable damage sustained in the past as a result of devastating slavery, which was, in turn, one of the forms of original accumulation of wealth in North America. Americans' present-day wealth is also built on blood and sweat of millions of African slaves, which some wish to easily forget but others should never forgive.

When a technocrat of Margrethe Vestager's class – seemingly one of the most competent European Commissioners – warns against the threat of takeover of European companies hit by the Covid-19 pandemic, this must make you wonder and worry. If a Chinese investor knocks to the door of entrepreneurs who are not coping well with the crisis, even with generous public aid from governments and European Commission, one needs to negotiate with him and strike a deal rather than shut the door in his face. Even if the Chinese take full control of some companies, this will be an inflow of fresh capital which is in short supply amid the crisis. This will often involve a transfer of high technologies, which are ever more abundant in China, and access on an ever larger scale to the Chinese market and to third markets. As a matter of fact, most of such investments will be oriented to production for exports. When Danish or German capital flows into Slovakia or Poland, these are desirable direct foreign investments, and when Chinese capital flows into Spain or Sweden, this is a "takeover of European firms"?

A fairly harmonized global order requires a strong and united European integration (Shambaugh, 2016), but unfortunately it is being weakened due to the financial and migration crisis and the growing wave of new nationalism and devolutionary tendencies. Brexit is further undermining the EU, reducing its economy by ca. 15 percent. Unfortunately, the European Union is becoming weaker at the time when it should gain strength to counterbalance China's growing influence. At the same time, the EU is China's leading cooperation partner and strategic rival; this is no contradiction but a sort of dialectic.

Against such backdrop, one should add another complication to this already complex equation: the triangle formed by China – Russia – the EU, notably Germany. The latter wants a strong, more deeply integrated European Union. It also wants good, pragmatic relations with both Russia and China. Now correct Russian-German relations are not being sought by Kaiser and his cousin, tsar, but by a chancellor and a president who speak its language. To both China is a vast market outlet; to Germany, for high-tech industrial products, to Russia, for raw materials, of which its land sprawling over eleven time zones has greater underground deposits than any other country. Geopolitical games played between those three have a major impact on the geoeconomic situation.

China cares about developing cooperation with other countries and regions, at the same time engaging them further in the globalization process. While the United States has over 200 military installations abroad in 120 countries, China has one – a small naval base in the Horn of Africa, in Djibouti – but, in contrast, is the largest trade partner for 130 countries. The sheer size of its economy makes it necessary to institutionalize foreign policy in the form of multilateral contacts. China must reach agreements at the bilateral level with countries like India or Russia but not with Tanzania or Argentina. This is why numerous forums have been created for communication and discussion, and sometimes for engaging in joint projects. Contacts with Africa are dealt with as part of Forum on China-Africa Cooperation (FOCAC), of which all of the continent's countries are members except Eswatini. To foster cooperation with the South America region, Forum of China and the Community of Latin American and Caribbean States (Foro China-CELAC)[28] was established. Organizations intended to strengthen contacts with immediate neighbours are China-South Asia Cooperation Forum (CSACF) and China-Central Asia Cooperation Forum (CCACF). There are more such institutions, because China does not lose sight of any world region – including

---

28. The Forum does not include the region's countries which maintain diplomatic relations with Taiwan, China: Belize, Guatemala, Haiti, Honduras, Nicaragua, Paraguay, Saint Kitts and Nevis, and Saint Lucia.

Oceania, the Arctic and the Antarctic. The functioning of those structures certainly brings multilateral benefits, and adds the "Chinese characteristics" to globalization.

Carrying out numerous projects requires finance. If their own funds are not enough, emancipating economies resort to foreign loans. China once used them, too, but at some point it became a lender, especially for developing economies, and now it is the largest creditor in the world. Loans granted by China, nearly none in 2000, in 2020 exceed the sum total of loans extended by the World Bank and the International Monetary Fund. At nearly 400 billion US dollars, they are twice as high as the official public debt of developing economies to the Paris Club countries. These amounts and relations between them are changing due to the pandemic-induced crisis because, on the one hand, both rich countries and China write off some of the irrecoverable debts of the so called Highly-Indebted Poor Countries[29] (HIPC), and, on the other, they extend new loans to those in need. The ongoing shifts in that area will strengthen China's

---

29. The Wold Bank classifies 39 economies as HIPC, as many as 33 of which in Sub-Saharan Africa: Benin, Burkina Faso, Burundi, Chad, Democratic Republic of the Congo, Eritrea, Ethiopia, Gambia, Ghana, Guinea, Guinea-Bissau, Cameroon, Comoros, the Congo, Ivory Coast, Liberia, Madagascar, Malawi, Mali, Mauretania, Mozambique, Niger, Senegal, Sierra Leone, Rwanda, Central African Republic, Somalia, Sudan, Tanzania, Togo, Uganda, São Tomé and Príncipe and Zambia; one in Asia, Afghanistan, and five in South and Central America and in the Caribbean – Bolivia, Guyana, Haiti, Honduras and Nicaragua (World Bank, 2020c).

position, especially that the White House's irresponsible policy discourages it from financing the US public debt. Part of the surplus that could have been placed in bonds of the wealthy United States will be invested in securities of economies working their way up. In the long run, it's a favourable structural change as it will boost the development of countries lagging behind, while – perhaps – partly motivating the USA to crack down on living beyond its means, which is financed with continuous borrowing.

Some believe that in the coming decades the main – not only economic – clash will be in the field of artificial intelligence, AI (Lee, 2018). In recent years China has made enormous headway in this sphere, using scientific and technological breakthroughs in electronic engineering and digitisation, as well as its unique position of having abundant Big Data. The bigger active population is, the larger the amount of data that helps build AI applications. In this specific respect only India can rival China. Meanwhile, the latter has still a lot to learn, and needs to create a more open innovation system (Medvedev, Piatkowski and Yusuf, 2020).

Considering the whole context – including the hardware and software quality, and especially highly-qualified professionals – the main competitive clash will, again, pit the United States against China. The ensuing economic tensions will become politicized, which can already be felt. It is beyond question that one of the reasons for the trade war and the new cold war initiated by Americans is this very fear of losing the AI supremacy. We are faced with two choices here: between a rivalry that upsets the equilibrium and dynamic, or cooperation and looking for synergies.

Since globalization can no longer be stopped, hence China's development, there will be an incessant debate on what is good and bad for the world. Yes, there are good and bad economies (Sedlacek, 2011), there are systems that are more and less effective in terms of meeting their objectives, there are progressive and backward ideologies and political systems that follow them. It is all the more important to learn as much as possible from one another and draw on the experience of others in a creative way. Anti-examples are also useful; if only to know what not to do. China has learnt a lot from others, while showing a unique capacity for approaching its problems from a pragmatic standpoint rather than an ideological one – the way it used to do. Nevertheless, it still needs to learn a lot. One should hope that it will be willing and able to.

Following the victorious, several decade-long war on poverty, it is in for another war, this time one to protect natural environment. Also this one can be won over time, and this will prove the *conditio sine qua non* of Chinism being accepted by next generations. Earlier on, China, and especially its leaders, were unwilling to sacrifice maximizing the traditionally defined (in the narrow quantitative terms) economic growth rate. Now – on the eve of being promoted to the group of high-income countries – it must sacrifice the same at the altar of development that is triply sustainable: economically, socially and environmentally. If it manages to do that, it will peacefully win another era on the never-ending path of development.

One of the most interesting comparative analyses of history was suggested by the British historian Ian Morris. He developed an original Social Development Index, which takes particular account of the energy capture, a given social culture's capacity for organization, measured with the size of its largest urban areas, war-making capacity and the advancement of information technology, determined by the speed and extent of the spread of the written word and telecommunications (Morris, 2010). Using those metrics, he reaches the conclusion that the West will keep dominating only for a couple of next generations after which, in the first decade of the 22nd century, the world will be dominated by the East, the most important part being, of course, China. Well, time will tell …

Long, long time ago – in the Mediterranean world that knew nothing of the Chinese civilization, though already back then smooth silk would be brought from there (Uhlig, 1986) – all roads led to Rome; *omnes viae Romam ducunt.* Is it now the time of *omnes viae Beijing ducunt?*

References

» Acemoglu, Daron and James A. Robinson (2012). *Why Nations Fail. The Origins of Power, Prosperity, and Poverty*, Crown Business, New York.

» Akerlof, George A., and Robert J. Shiller (2015). *Phishing for Phools: The Economics of Manipulation and Deception*, Princeton University Press, Princeton, NY.

» Arthur, W. Brian (2015). *Complexity of the Economy*, Oxford University Press, Oxford – New York.

» Atkinson, Anthony B. (2018). *Inequality: What Can Be Done?*, Harvard University Press, Cambridge, Mass.

» Bremmer, Ian (2010). *The End of the Free Market: Who Wins the War Between States and Corporations?*, Portfolio, New York.

» Brown, Kerry (2019). *What Does China Want? China's World*, I. B. Tauris, London - New York.

» Brunnermeier, Markus K., Harold James and Jean-Pierre Landau (2016). *The Euro and the Battles of Ideas*, Princeton University Press, Princeton and Oxford.

» CB (2020). *The Conference Board Total Economy Database*, The Conference Board, April (https://www.conference-board.org/data/economy-database/index. cfm?id=27762).

» China Daily (2017). *Xi Jinping and His Era*, "China Daily", November 18–19.

» CNBC (2020). '*A bill has to come due for China*': *White House advisor Navarro threatens coronavirus retaliation*, "CNBC. Politics", May 11
(https://www.cnbc.com/2020/ 05/11/coronavirus-trump-advisor-navarro-threatens-retaliation-against-china.html).

» Cooper, George (2014). *Money, Blood and Revolution: How Darwin and the doctor of King Charles I could turn economics into a science*, Harriman House, Petersfield, Hampshire.

» Csaba, Laszlo (1996). *The Political Economy of the Reform Strategy: China and Eastern Europe Compared*, "Communist Economies and Economic Transformations", Vol. 8 (1), p. 53-65
(https://www.tandfonline.com/doi/abs/10.1080/146313796084 27844).

» Csaba, *László* (2009). *Crisis in Economics?*, Akadémiai Kiadó, Budapest.

» Csaba, László (2019). *Unorthodoxy in Hungary: an illiberal success story?*, "Post-Communist Economies"
(https://www.tandfonline.com/doi/full/10.1080/14631377.2019. 1641949).

» Deneen, Patrick J. (2018). *Why Liberalism Failed*, Yale University Press, New Haven and London.

» Economist (2012). *True progressivism*, "The Economist", October 13.

» Economist (2016). *The new nationalism*, "The Economist", November 19 (https://www.economist.com/leaders/ 2016/11/19/the-new-nationalism).

» Economist (2019a). *What companies are for: Big business is beginning to accept broader social responsibilities*, "The Economist", August 24
(https://www.economist.com/briefing/2019/08/22/big-business-is-beginning-to-accept-broader-social-responsibilities).

» Economist (2019b). *I'm from a company and I'm here to help: The case for more state spending on R&D*, "The Economist", August 24
(https://www.economist.com/briefing/2021/01/16/the-case-for-more-state-spending-on-r-and-d).

» Economist (2019c). *Warrensworld: Elizabeth Warren's many plans would reshape American capitalism*, "The Economist", October 24
(https://www.economist.com/briefing/2019/10/24/elizabeth-warrens-many-plans-would-reshape-american-capitalism).

» Economist (2020a). *The pandemic is driving America and China further apart*, "The Economist", May 9
(https://www.economist.com/leaders/2020/05/09/the-pandemic-is-driving-america-and-china-further-apart).

» Economist (2020b). *There is less trust between Washington and Beijing than at any point since 1979*, "The Economist", May 9
(https://www.economist.com/united-states/2020/05/09/there-is-less-trust-between-washington-and-beijing-than-at-any-point-since-1979).

» Economist (2020c). *Has covid-19 killed globalisation?*, "The Economist", May 16 (https://www.economist.com/leaders/2020/05/14/has-covid-19-killed-globalisation).

» Economy, Elizabeth C. (2018). *The Third World Revolution: Xi Jinping and the New Chinese State*, Oxford University Press, New York.

» EU (2020). *European Economic Forecast*, "Institutional Paper 25", European Commission, Brussels. (https://ec.europa.eu/info/sites/info/files/economy-finance/ip125_en.pdf).

» Financial Times (2017). *Xi Jinping signals departure from low-profile policy*, "Financial Times", October 20 (https://www.ft.com/content/05cd86a6-b552-11e7-a398-73d59db9e399).

» Forbes (2020). *The World's Most Valuable Brands*, "Forbes" (https://www.forbes.com/powerful-brands/list/#tab:rank).

» Friedman, Milton (1970). *The Social Responsibility of Business Is to Increase its Profits*, "The New York Times Magazine", September 13 (http://umich.edu/~thecore/doc/Friedman.pdf).

» Galbraith, John K. (1958). *The Affluent Society*, Houghton Mifflin, Boston.

» Galbraith, James K. (2014). *The End of Normal: The Great Crisis and the Future of Growth*, Simon and Schuster, New York.

» Galbraith, James K. (2018). *Backwater Economics and New Pragmatism: Institutions and Evolution in the Search for a Sustainable Economics*, "TIGER Working Papers Series", No. 138, Kozminski University, Warsaw

(http://www.tiger.edu.pl/TWP%20No.%20138%20–%20Galbraith.
pdf).

» Galbraith, James K. (2019a). *The Pragmatism of John Kenneth Galbraith*, "Acta Oeconomica", Vol. 69, Special Issue 1, p. 195-213
(https://akjournals.com/view/journals/032/69/s1/article-p195.xml).

» Galbraith, James K. (2019b). *Old and New Pragmatism: Challenges and Opportunities for Economics*. Lecture presented at the inauguration of academic year 2019-2020, Department of Economics, Gdansk University, September 30
(https://www.youtube.com/watch?reload=9&v=YwMbra5XWIk&fe
ature=youtu.be).

» Galbraith, James K. (2019c). *Klucz do stworzenia egalitarnego społeczeństwa [The key to creating an egalitarian society]*, "Rzeczpospolita. Plus Minus", November 23-24, p. 14-16 (in Polish).

» Gunn, Giles (1992). *Thinking Across the American Grain: Ideology, Intellect, and the New Pragmatism*, The University of Chicago Press, London.

» Harvey, David (2005). *A Brief History of Neoliberalism*, Oxford University Press, Oxford - New York.

» Harvey, David (2015). *Seventeen Contradictions and the End of Capitalism*, Profile Books, London.

» Huang, Yukon (2017). *Cracking the China Conundrum: Why Conventional Economic Wisdom Is Wrong*, Oxford University Press, New York.

» Kahneman, Daniel (2011). *Thinking, Fast and Slow*, Farrar, Strauss and Giroux, New York.

» Kessler, Sarah (2018). *Gigged: The Gig Economy, the End of the Job and the Future of Work*, St. Martin Press, New York.

» King, Stephen D. (2013). *When the Money Runs Out. The End of Western Affluence*, Yale University Press, New Haven and London.

» Kissinger, Henry (2011). *On China*, Penguin Press, New York.

» Klein, Matthew C. and Michael Petts (2020). *Trade Wars are Class Wars: How Rising Inequality Distorts the Global Economy and Threatens International Peace*, Yale University Press, New Haven and London.

» Kolodko, Grzegorz W. (2000). *From Shock to Therapy: The Political Economy of Postsocialist Transformation*, Oxford University Press, Oxford - New York.

» Kolodko, Grzegorz W. (2011). *Truth, Errors and Lies. Politics and Economics in a Volatile World*, Columbia University Press, New York.

» Kolodko, Grzegorz W. (2014a). *Whither the World: The Political Economy of the Future*, Palgrave Macmillan, Houndmills, Basingstoke, Hampshire and New York.

» Kolodko, Grzegorz W. (2014b). *The New Pragmatism, or Economics and Policy for the Future*, "Acta Oeconomica", Vol. 64 (2), p. 139-160 (http://tiger.edu.pl/aktualnosci/2014/acta-ocevonomica-64-2014.pdf).

» Kolodko, Grzegorz W. (2018). *Socialism, Capitalism, or Chinism?*, "Communist and Post-Communist Studies", Vol. 51 (4), p. 285-298
(http://tiger.edu.pl/CPCS_2018.pdf).

» Kolodko, Grzegorz W. (2020a). *China and the Future of Globalization: The Political Economy of China's Rise*, Bloomsbury I. B. Tauris, London – New York – Oxford – New Delhi – Sydney.

» Kolodko, Grzegorz W. (2020b). *Economics and politics of post-communist transition to market and democracy: The Lessons from Polish experience*, "Post-Communist Economies", Vol. 32 (3), p. 285-305
(https://doi.org/10.1080/14631377.2019.1694604).

» Kolodko, Grzegorz W. (2020c). *After the Calamity: Economics and Politics of the Post-Pandemic World*, "Polish Sociological Review", No. 2 (210), p. 137-155
(http://tiger.edu.pl/After_the_Calamity.pdf).

» Kolodko, Grzegorz W. (2021). *The Quest for Development Success: Bridging Theoretical Reasoning with Economic Practice*, Lexington Books Rowman & Littlefield, Lanham –Boulder – New York – London.

» Kolodko, Grzegorz W. and Michal Rutkowski (1991). *The Problem of Transition from a Socialist to a Free Market Economy: The Case of Poland*, "The Journal of Social, Political and Economic Studies", Vol. 16 (2), p. 159-179
(http://www.tiger.edu.pl/kolodko/artykuly/The_Problem.pdf).

» Koźmiński, Andrzej K., Adam Noga, Katarzyna Piotrowska, Krzysztof Zagórski (2020). *The Balanced Development Index for Europe's OECD Countries, 1999-2017*, Springer Briefs in Economics, Springer, Cham, Switzerland.

» Krastev, Ivan and Stephen Holmes (2019). *The Light That Failed: Why the West Is Losing the Fight for Democracy*, Pegasus Books, New York - London.

» Krugman, Paul (2020). *Arguing with Zombies: Economics, Politics, and the Fight for a Better Future*, W. W. Norton and Company, New York.

» Kuenzler, Adrian (2017). *Restoring Consumer Sovereignty: How Markets Manipulate Us and What the Law Can Do About It*, Oxford University Press, New York.

» Lankov, Andrei (2013). *The Real North Korea: Life and Politics in the Failed Stalinist Utopia*, Oxford University Press, New York.

» Lardy, Nicholas R. (2014). *Markets Over Mao: The Rise of Private Business in China*, Peterson Institute of International Economies, Washington, DC.

» Lardy, Nicholas R. (2019). *The State Strikes Back: The End of Economic Reform in China?*, Peterson Institute of International Economics, Washington, DC.

» Lee, Kai-Fu (2018). *AI Superpowers: China, Silicon Valley, and the New World Order*, Houghton Mifflin Harcourt, Boston, Mass.

» Lin, Justin Yifu (2012a). *Demystifying the Chinese Economy*, Cambridge University Press, Cambridge.

» Lin, Justin Yifu (2012b). *New Structural Economics: A Framework for Rethinking Development and Policy*, The World Bank, Washington, DC.

» Lin, Justin Yifu (2013). *Against the Consensus: Reflections on the Great Recession*, Cambridge University Press, New York.

» Macrotrends (2020). *Macrotrends – The Premier Research Platform for Long Term Investors*
(https://www.macro-trends.net/).

» Maçães, Bruno (2018). *Belt and Road: A Chinese World Order*, Hurts, London.

» Mao Zedong (1974). *Chairman Mao Zedong's Theory on the Division of the Three World and the Strategy of Forming an Alliance Against an Opponent*, The Ministry of Foreign Affairs of the Republic of China
(https://www.fmprc.gov.cn/mfa_eng/ziliao_665539/3602_665543/3604_665547/t18008.shtml).

» Medvedev, Denis, Marcin Piatkowski, Shahid Yusuf (2020). *Promoting Innovation in China: Lessons from International Good Practice*, The World Bank Group, Washington, DC
(http://documents.worldbank.org/curated/en/571611587708038991/pdf/Promoting-Innovation-in-China-Lessons-from-International-Good-Practice.pdf).

» Milanovic, Branko (2011). *The Haves and the Have-Nots: A Brief and Idiosyncratic History of Global Inequality*, Basic Books, New York.

» Milanovic, Branko (2016). *Global Inequality for the Age of Globalization*, The Belknap Press of Harvard University Press, Cambridge, Massachusetts – London, England.

» Milanovic, Branko (2019). *Capitalism, Alone: The Future of the System That Rules the World*, Harvard University Press, Cambridge, Mass.

» Minxin, Pei (2016). *China's Crony Capitalism: The Dynamics of Regime Decay*, Harvard University Press, Cambridge, Massachusetts – London, England.

» Morris, Ian (2010). *Why the West Rules – for Now: The Patterns of History and What They Reveal about the Future*, Profile Books, London.

» Nuti, D. Mario (2018). *The Rise and Fall of Socialism*, Dialogue of Civilizations Research Institute, Berlin (https://doc-research.org/wp-content/uploads/2019/01/The-rise-and-fall-of-socialism_Download-file.pdf).

» Obbema, Fokke (2015). *China and the West: Hope and Fear in the Age of Asia*, I. B. Tauris, London – New York.

» PAP (2020). USA: *Chiny powinny wypłacić St. Zjedn. odszkodowanie za COVID-19*, Polska Agencja Prasowa (Polish Press Agency), May 12 (in Polish) (https://www.obserwatorfinansowy.pl/forma/dispatches/usa-chiny-powinny-wyplacic-st-zjedn-odszkodowanie-za-covid-19/).

» Pei, Minxin (2016). *China's Crony Capitalism: The Dynamics of Regime Decay*, Harvard University Press, Cambridge, Massachusetts – London.

» Phelps, Edmund S. (2013). *Mass Flourishing: How Grassroots Innovation Created Jobs, Challenge, and Change*, Princeton University Press, New York.

» Piatkowski, Marcin (2018). *Europe's Growth Champion: Insights from the Economic Rise of Poland*, Oxford University Press, Oxford.

» Ridley, Matt (2010). *The Rational Optimist: How Prosperity Evolves*, Harper – Collins, New York.

» Rodrik, Dani (2015). *Economics Rules: Why Economics Works, When It Fails, and How To Tell The Difference*, Oxford University Press, Oxford.

» Roland, Gerard (2019). *Coexisting with China in the 21st Century*, "Acta Oeconomica", Vol. 69, Special Issue 1, p. 49-70
(https://akjournals.com/view/journals/032/69/s1/article-p49.xml).

» Rosling, Hans, Ola Rosling and Anna Rosling Ronnlund (2018). *Factfulness: Ten Reasons We're Wrong About the World – and Why Things Are Better than You Think*, Flatiron Book, New York.

» QS (2020). *QS. World University Ranking: Who Rules?*, QS Top Universities
(https://www.topuniversities.com/university-rankings/world-university-rankings/2020).

» Saez, Emmanuel and Gabriel Zucman (2019). *The Triumph of Injustice: How the Rich Dodge Taxes and How to Make Them Pay*, W. W. Norton & Company, New York.

» Sedlacek, Tomas (2011). *Economics of Good and Evil: The Quest for Economic Meaning from Gilgamesh to Wall Street*, Oxford University Press, Oxford – New York.

» Shambaugh, David (2016). *China's Future*, Polity Press, Cambridge, UK – Malden, MD.

» Skidelsky, Robert (2020). *What's Wrong with Economics? A Primer for the Perplexed*, Yale University Press, New Haven and London.

» Sloman, Steven and Philip Fernbach (2017). *The Knowledge Illusion: Why We Never Think Alone*, Riverhead Books, New York.

» Stiglitz, Joseph E. (2019a). *People, Power, and Profits: Progressive Capitalism for an Age of Discontent*, W. W. Norton, New York – London.

» Stiglitz, Joseph E. (2019b). *Progressive Capitalism Is Not an Oxymoron. We can save our broken economic system from itself,* "The New York Times", April 19
(https://www.nytimes.com/2019/04/19/opinion/sunday/progressive-capitalism.html).

» Stiglitz, Joseph C. (2019c). *Can we trust CEOs' shock conversion to corporate benevolence?,* "The Guardian", August 29
(https://www.theguardian.com/business/2019/aug/29/can-we-trust-ceos-shock-conversion-to-corporate-benevolence).

» Stein, Jeff, Carol D. Leonnig, Josh Dawsey and Gerry Shih (2020). *U.S. officials crafting retaliatory actions against China over coronavirus as President Trump fumes,* "Washington Post", May 1
(https://www.washingtonpost.com/business/2020/04/30/trump-china-coronavirus-retaliation/).

» Stiglitz, Joseph E., Jean-Paul Fitoussi i Martine Durand (2019). *Beyond GDP: Measuring What Counts for Economic and Social Performance*, Organization for Economic Cooperation and Development, Paris.

» Sun, Feng, Wanfa Zhang (2020). *Why Communist China isn't Collapsing: The CCP's Battle for Survival and State-Society Dynamics in the Post-Reform Era*, Lexington Books

Rowman & Littlefield, Lanham - Boulder - New York - London.

» Sundararajan, Arun (2017). *The Sharing Economy: The End of Employment and the Rise of Crowd-Based Capitalism*, MIT Press, Cambridge, Mass.

» Tanzi, Vito (2018). *The Ecology of Tax Systems: Factors That Shape the Demand and Supply of Taxes*, Edward Elgar, Cheltenham.

» Thaler, Richard H. (2016). *Misbehaving: The Making of Behavioral Economics*, W. W. Norton & Company, New York.

» Thaler, Richard H. and Cass R. Sunstein (2009). *Nudge: Improving Decisions About Health, Wealth, and Happiness*, Penguin Books, London.

» Tirole, Jean (2017). *Economics of the Common Good*, Princeton University Press, Princeton, New Jersey.

» Trade Map (2020). *Trade Map. Trade statistics for international business development* (www.trademap.org/Country_SelProductCountry.aspx?nvpm=1%7c 156%7c%7c%7c%7cTOTAL%7c%7c%7c%7c2%7c1%7c1%7c1%7c1%7c %7c2%7c1%7c).

» Uhlig, Helmut (1986). *Die Seidenstrasse. Antike Weltkultur zwischen China und Rom*, Lübbe, Bergisch Gladbach (in German).

» UN (2019). *World Population Prospects 2019*, United Nations, Department of Economic and Social Affairs, Populations Dynamic, New York (https://population.un.org/wpp/Download/Probabilistic/ Population/).

» UNDP (2019). *Human Development Report: Beyond income, beyond averages, beyond today: Inequalities in human development in the 21st century*, United Nations Development Programme, New York
(http://www.hdr.undp.org/sites/default/files/hdr2019.pdf).

» Walicki, Andrzej (1995). *Marxism and the Leap to the Kingdom of Freedom: The Rise and Fall of the Communist Utopia*, Stanford University Press, Stanford.

» Warren, Elizabeth (2018). *This Fight Is Our Fight: The Battle to Save America's Middle Class*, Metropolitan Books, New York.

» WEF (2019). *The Global Competitiveness Report 2019*, World Economic Forum, Geneva
(http://www3.weforum.org/docs/WEF_TheGlobalCompetitiveness
Report2019.pdf).

» WEO (2019). *World Economic Outlook*, October, International Monetary Fund, Washington, DC
(https://knoema.com/IMFWEO2019Oct/imf-world-economic-
outlook-weo-october-2019).

» WEO (2020). *World Economic Outlook, April 2020: The Great Lockdown*, International Monetary Fund, Washington, DC
(https://www.imf.org/en/Publications/WEO/Issues/2020/04/14/
weo-april-2020).

» Wiatr, Jerzy J. (2019). *New Authoritarianism: Challenges to Democracy in the 21st Century*, Verlag Barbara Budrich, Opladen –Berlin – Toronto.

» World Bank (2020a). *The World Bank in China*, The World Bank, Washington, DC
(https://www.worldbank.org/en/country/china/overview).

» World Bank (2020b). *World Bank. International Comparison Program database*, The World Bank, Washington, DC
(https://data.worldbank.org/indicator/NY.GDP.MKTP.PP.CD).

» World Bank (2020c). *Heavily indebted poor countries (HIPIC)*, The World Bank, Washington DC
(https://data.worldbank.org/region/heavily-indebted-poor-countries-hipc).

» Xi, Jinping (2014). *The Governance of China*, ICP Intercultural Press, Beijing.

» Zelizer (2015). *The Fierce Urgency of Now: Lyndon Johnson, Congress, and the Battle for the Great Society*, Penguin Books, New York.

Author's Publications in the Chinese Language

1. 《波兰前副总理解析中国－中东欧合作：看好后疫情时期发展，建议着眼"智慧投资"》(Analysis of China-CEEC cooperation by Former Deputy Premier of Poland: optimistic about post-pandemic developments, recommend more "smart investing"), China News Service, February 9, 2021.

   https://mp.weixin.qq.com/s/mYHx7XGqUSALmkEAFiV59g

2. 《中国为全球提供国家治理解决方案》(China provides national governance solutions for the world), China Publishing and Media Journal, February 2, 2021.

   http://tiger.edu.pl/ChinaPublishingandMediaJournal_02.02.2021.pdf

3. 《疫情后的世界经济和政治》(Economics and Politics in the Post-Pandemic World), Social Sciences Abroad, 2020, No. 5, p. 73-82.

4. 《疫情如何加剧百年未有之大变局》(How the Pandemic Accelerates the Changes Unseen in a Century), Guangming Daily, July 7th, 2020.

   http://epaper.gmw.cn/gmrb/html/2020-07/07/nw.D110000gmrb_20200707_1-12.htm?from=singlemessage

5. 《波兰前副总理、北师大特聘教授：四路径重塑疫情过后世界新秩序》(The former deputy prime minister of

Poland and BNU distinguished professor: Better paths needed to help shape the future), "BNU News", May 1, 2020.

http://news.bnu.edu.cn/zx/zhxw/116509.htm

6. 《波兰前副总理：后疫情时代 更加双赢的全球化》(The former Deputy Prime Minister of Poland: a more win-win globalization in the post-epidemic era), Guangming Daily, April 17th, 2020.

http://news.gmw.cn/2020-04/17/content_33746142.htm

7. 《中国能否拯救世界？》(Will China Save the World?), Encyclopedia of China Publishing House, Beijing, January 2020.

8. 《欧元区扩大的决定性因素与影响》(Decisive Factors and Impacts of Eurozone Expansion), Chinese Journal of European Studies, 2018, No. 3, p. 1-23.

http://www.tiger.edu.pl/Euro_.pdf

9. 《新自由主义正在给美国经济酝酿危机》(Neoliberalism is Brewing a Crisis for the U.S. Economy), China Economic Weekly, January 22, 2018, p. 82-83.

http://www.tiger.edu.pl/US%20tax.pdf

10. 《新自由主义对未来世界的"诅咒"》(The "Curse" of Neoliberalism for the Future World), Global Times, January 18, 2018.

http://opinion.huanqiu.com/hqpl/2018-01/11532453.html

11. 《新自由主义 2.0 成为美国及世界经济新诅咒》(Neo-liberalism 2.0 is Becoming a New Curse for the U.S. and the World Economy), FTchinese.com, January 18, 2018.

http://www1.ftchinese.com/story/001075977?page=1

12. 《新自由主义 2.0 方兴未艾 成为美国及世界经济新诅咒》 (Neoliberalism 2.0 is Still Developing and is Becoming a New Curse for the U.S. and the World Economy), Center for China and Globalization, January 12, 2018.
http://mp.weixin.qq.com/s/hdw6HYTH5gVbKZZmHY1iPw

13. 《如何毁灭一个国家 —— 希腊危机的经济学与政治学》 (How to Destroy a Country: Economics and Politics of the Greek Crisis), Journal of Translation from Foreign Literature of Economics, 2017, Vol. 173, No. 3, p. 27-41.
http://www.tiger.edu.pl/In%20Chinese_Chinese_How%20to%20Destroy%20a%20Country%20The%20Economics%20and%20Politics%20of%20Greek%20Crisis.pdf

14. 《全球化浪潮中，中国发挥的积极作用日益瞩目》 (China's Active Role in Globalization is Increasingly Prominent), China Economic Weekly, June 5, 2017, p. 84-85.
http://www.tiger.edu.pl/WillChinaSavetheWorld_VI2017.pdf

15. 《把握新实用主义和中庸经济学，实现可持续发展》 (Master New Pragmatism and Golden Mean Economics to Achieve Sustainable Development), China Economic Weekly, January 16, 2017.
http://www.tiger.edu.pl/2017.01.16_New%20Pragmatism.pdf

16. 《新实用主义 —— "一带一路"倡议的理论基石》 (New Pragmatism: The Theoretical Cornerstone of the Belt and Road Initiative), International Symposium on Green Development and Global Governance, November 14, 2016.
http://www.tiger.edu.pl/2_Pragmatism%20as%20the%20Theoretical%20Foundation%20for%20One%20Belt,%20One%20Road%20Initiative_Chinese%20Translation_14.XI.pdf

17. 《全球治理变革与中波关系高端对话》(Change in Global Governance and High-end Dialogue between China and Poland), lecture at Hangzhou University of Science and Technology (HUST), November 9, 2016.

http://www.tiger.edu.pl/1_Changing%20Global%20Governance%20and%20The%20Relationship%20between%20China%20and%20Poland_10.XI.pdf

18. 《中国经济没有硬着陆》(China's Economy Has not Entered into "Hard landing"), International Seminar on the Belt and Road Initiative Theming on "Shared Memory, Common Development", September 26-27, 2016.

http://www.tiger.edu.pl/kolodko/kolodko/referaty/pl/KOLODKO_Xian%20paper%20in%20Chinese.pdf

19. 《英国脱欧或引发连锁危机，世界又该何去何从?》(Brexit May Trigger a Chain Crisis, Whither the World?), China Economic Weekly, August 8, 2016.

http://www.tiger.edu.pl/kolodko/artykuly/Brexitology_CEW_08.08.16.pdf

20. 《21世纪政治经济学：世界将去向何方》(The Political Economy of the Future), Central Compilation and Translation Press, 2015.

21. 《人均 GDP 与人类发展指数哪个更准确》(新兴市场或者解放经济), (Which is More Accurate, GDP per Capita or Human Development Index — Emerging Markets or Emancipating Economy), China Economic Weekly, April 21, 2014, p. 84-85.

http://www.tiger.edu.pl/kolodko/artykuly/Brexitology_CEW_08.08.16.pdf

22. 《中国经济不会硬着陆》(China's Economy will not Enter into "hard landing"), China Economic Weekly, December 9, 2013, p. 86-87.

http://www.tiger.edu.pl/kolodko/artykuly/chinsku/China-2013-12.pdf

23. 《小心经济领域中的"预言家"》 (Watch Out for "Prophets" in the Economic Realm), China Economic Weekly, November 25, 2013, p. 82-83.

http://www.tiger.edu.pl/kolodko/artykuly/chinsku/China-2013-11.pdf.

24. 《新实用主义或经济学及未来政策》(New Pragmatism or Economics and Future Policy), Cai Jing Magazine, 2013, No. 30 (October 28), p. 30-34.

http://www.tiger.edu.pl/kolodko/artykuly/chinsku/China- 2013-10-1.pdf

25. 《全球进入收入分配不公最严重时期》(The World has Entered the Worst Period of Income Inequality), China Economic Weekly, No. 21, October 2013, p. 84-85.

http://www.tiger.edu.pl/kolodko/artykuly/chinsku/China-2013-10.pdf

26. 《当前的世界经济危机可在 30 年前避免》 (The Current World Economic Crisis Can be Avoided 30 Years Ago), China Economic Weekly, September 23, 2013, p. 86-87.

http://tiger.edu.pl/kolodko/artykuly/chinsku/China-2013-09.pdf

27. 《新兴经济体如何成为"自主经济体"？》(How do Emerging Economies Become "Autonomous Economies"?), China Economic Weekly, August 19, 2013, p. 84-85.

http://tiger.edu.pl/kolodko/artykuly/chinsku/China-2013-08.pdf

28. 《不道德的经济学家》(Immoral Economist), China Economic Weekly, July 15, 2013, p. 86-87.

http://tiger.edu.pl/kolodko/artykuly/chinsku/China-2013-07.pdf

29. 《经济学为什么不诚实》(Why Economics is Dishonest), China Economic Weekly, June 26, 2013, p. 86-87.

http://tiger.edu.pl/kolodko/artykuly/chinsku/2013-06.pdf

30. 《我们需要均衡的经济学》(We Need Balanced Economics), China Economic Weekly, May 20, 2013, p. 86-87.

http://tiger.edu.pl/kolodko/artykuly/chinsku/2013-05.pdf

31. 《主流经济学过时了》(Mainstream Economics is Outdated), China Economic Weekly, April 15, 2013, p. 86-87.

http://tiger.edu.pl/kolodko/artykuly/chinsku/2013-04.pdf

32. 《收入分配变革应惠及大众》(Changes in Income Distribution Should Benefit the Public), China Economic Weekly, March 25, 2013, p. 86-87.

http://tiger.edu.pl/kolodko/artykuly/chinsku/2013-03-03.pdf

33. 《地区一体化是全球化最好机遇》(Regional Integration Offers the Best Opportunity for Globalization), China Economic Weekly, February 25, 2013, p. 86-87.

http://tiger.edu.pl/kolodko/artykuly/chinsku/2013-2-China.pdf

34. 《第四次工业革命何时到来》(When Will the 4th Industrial Revolution Arrive), China Economic Weekly, January 14, 2013, p. 86-87.

http://tiger.edu.pl/kolodko/artykuly/chinsku/2013-1-China.pdf

35. 《欧盟的"七年计划"为何不完美》（"市场和计划"）(Why the EU's "Seven Year Plan" is not Perfect) (Market and Planning), China Economic Weekly, December 24, 2012, p. 20-21.

http://tiger.edu.pl/kolodko/artykuly/12_Market_and_Planning_CEW_12.pdf

36. 《落实企业社会责任需"胡萝卜加大棒"》（经济—想法与实践）("Carrots and Sticks" Needed for Implementing Corporate Social Responsibility) (Economy – Ideas and Practice), China Economic Weekly, November 26, 2012, p. 20-21.

http://tiger.edu.pl/kolodko/artykuly/11_Economy-Ideas_and_Practice%20_CEW_11.pdf

37. 《未来全球经济更应看中幸福指数》（"实用主义"）(The Future Global Economy Should Put More Emphasis on the Happiness Index) ("New Pragmatism"), China Economic Weekly, October 15, 2012, p. 20-21.

http://www.tiger.edu.pl/kolodko/artykuly/10_NewPragmatism_CEW_10.pdf

38. 《"新自由主义救全球化"是特殊利益集团的骗局》（发展的三个平衡关系：价值观、制度、政策）("Neoliberalism Can Save Globalization" is a Scam by Special Interest Groups) (Development Triangle: Values, Institutions, and Policies), China Economic Weekly, September 10, 2012, p. 18-19.

http://www.tiger.edu.pl/kolodko/artykuly/9_DevelopmentTriangle_CEW_9.pdf

39. 《古巴改革：别把孩子同洗澡水一起倒掉》(Cuba Reform: Do not Dump the Baby Together with the Bath Water), China Economic Weekly, August 6, 2012, p. 22-23.

http://www.tiger.edu.pl/kolodko/artykuly/8_Cuba_CEW_8.pdf

40. 《中东北非的艰难时刻才刚刚开始》(The Difficult Times for Middle East and North Africa have just

Begun), China Economic Weekly, July 2, 2012, p. 20-21.
http://tiger.edu.pl/kolodko/artykuly/chinsku/7_The_Arab_
Awakening_CEW_7.pdf

41. 《乌克兰：在东、西之间艰难抉择》(Ukraine: Difficult
Choice between East and West), China Economic
Weekly, June 18, 2012, p. 22-23.
http://tiger.edu.pl/kolodko/artykuly/Kolodko_Kuda_idiet_Rossija_
Efektivnoje_Antikrizisnoje_Uprawlenije_No_3_2012.pdf

42. 《未来十年，俄罗斯须向中国学习》(Russia Needs to
Learn from China in the Next Decade), China Economic
Weekly, May 21, 2012, p. 20-21.
http://www.tiger.edu.pl/kolodko/artykuly/chinsku/5_Whither_
Russia_CEW_5.pdf

43. 《"开罗共识"不是追求革命》("Cairo Consensus" is
not a Pursuit of Revolution), China Economic Weekly,
April 9, 2012, p. 30-31.

44. 《给希腊的千亿援助是场灾难》(100 Billion Aid to
Greece is a Disaster), China Economic Weekly, March 5,
2012, p. 20-21.
http://www.tiger.edu.pl/kolodko/artykuly/chinsku/the_greek_
syndrome_cew_3.pdf

45. 《欧洲债国何不拿外储还债?》(Why European Debtor
Nations Do not Pay Off Their Debts with Foreign
Reserves?), China Economic Weekly, February 6, 2012, p.
24-25.
http://www.tiger.edu.pl/kolodko/artykuly/chinsku/Unorthodox_
Crisis_Calls_for_Unorthodox_Action_CEW_2.pdf

46. 《新自由主义、世界危机与出路》(Neoliberalism,
World Crisis, and Ways Out), China Economic Weekly,

January 30, 2012, p. 20-21.

http://www.tiger.edu.pl/kolodko/artykuly/chinsku/Neoliberalism_
the_World_Crisis_and_Ways_Out_CEW_1.pdf

47. 《真相谬误与谎言：多变世界中的政治与经济》(Truth, Errors, and Lies: Politics and Economics in a Volatile World), Foreign Languages Press, Beijing, November 2011.

48. 《新自由主义与世界经济危机》(Neoliberalism and the World Economic Crisis), Russian Studies, 2010, No. 2 (162), p. 3-11.

http://www.tiger.edu.pl/kolodko/artykuly/chinsku/Two_Decades_
of_Transformation_RUSSIAN_STUDIES_No_2_2010.pdf

49. 《新自由主义、全球危机及其出路》(Neoliberalism, the Global Crisis, and the Ways Out), Comparative Studies, 2010, No. 3, p. 111-118.

http://www.tiger.edu.pl/kolodko/artykuly/chinsku/BIJIAO_
N0_3_2010_Neoliberalism.pdf

50. 《1989-2029 年大转型——可以更好或将会更好吗？》(The Great Transformation 1989-2029: Can It be Better, Will It be Better?), Russian Studies, 2009, No. 3 (157), p. 14-28.

http://www.tiger.edu.pl/kolodko/artykuly/chinsku/Great_Trans-
formation_1989-2029_RUSSIAN_STUIDES_No._3_2009.pdf

51. 《制度、政策和发展》中国公共服务体制：中央与地方关系 (Institutions, Policies, and Development), in: (Public Service Systems in China: Relationship Between the Central and Local Governments), Proceedings of China Institute for Reform and Development (CIRD), October 28-29, 2006, p. 401-411.

http://www.tiger.edu.pl/aktualnosci/haikou.doc

52. 《新兴市场应从波兰大变革中汲取的经验教训》(Lessons for the Emerging Markets from the Great Changes in Poland), Comparative Economic and Social Systems, 2005, No. 5, p. 28-33.

http://www.tiger.edu.pl/aktualnosci/bijao.pdf

53. 《新兴市场应从波兰大变革中汲取的经验教训》(Lessons for the Emerging Markets from the Great Changes in Poland), China Reform Summit, Promoting Economic Restructuring through Administrative Reforms, July 12-13, 2005.

http://www.tiger.edu.pl/aktualnosci/bijao.pdf

54. 《制度、政策和增长》(Institutions, Policies and Growth), Comparative Studies, 2005, No. 18 (May 21), p. 131-149.

http://www.tiger.edu.pl/aktualnosci/bijao.pdf

55. 《并非"小政府、大社会"就一定适合中国》("Small Government, Big Society"is not Necessarily Suitable for China), China Social News, December 2, 2004, p. 2.

http://www.tiger.edu.pl/kolodko/wywiady/China_Oriental_Outlook.pdf

56. 《向市场经济转轨：渐进主义与激进主义》(Transition to a Market Economy: Gradualism and Radicalism), Finance and Economics, Southwestern University of Finance and Economics (SWUFE), Chengdu, November 2004, p. 15-19 (The English version of the Manuscript was Authorized on March 10, 2004, after Professor Kolodko Received an Honorary Doctorate from the Chengdu University).

http://www.tiger.edu.pl/kolodko/wystapienia/chengdu_cn.lecture.pdf

57. 《"我是中国经济的推销者"》(I Am Popularizing the Chinese Economy), Hainan Daily , November 1, 2004 (Interview).

http://www.tiger.edu.pl/kolodko/wywiady/hainandaily.01112004.pdf

58. 《制度、政策和增长》(Institution, Policies and Growth), International Forum on China's Reform, October 30, 2004.

http://www.tiger.edu.pl/kolodko/artykuly/chinsku/chinareform.102004.pdf

59. 《全球化与后社会主义国家大预测》(The World Economy And Great Post-Communist Change), World Affairs Press, Beijing, June 2003.

60. 《全球化和转轨，幻想和现实》(Globalization and Transition, Fantasy and Reality), International Symposium on Comparison of Institutional Arrangements in Transitional Economies, Haikou, China, June 10-12, 2002.

http://www.tiger.edu.pl/kolodko/artykuly/chinsku/Haikou.pdf

61. 《从休克到治疗：后社会主义转轨的政治经济》(From Shock to Therapy: The Political Economy of Postsocialist Transformation), Far East Press, Shanghai, January 2000.

62. 《转轨国家向市场和企业家精神的转变》(Transforming Nations' Transition to Markets and Entrepreneurship), Comparative Economic and Social Systems, 2000, No. 3, p. 61-71.

http://www.tiger.edu.pl/kolodko/artykuly/2000_3.pdf

63. 《从"休克"失败到"后华盛顿共识"》(From the Fail of "Shock" to "Post-Washington Consensus"), Comparative Economic and Social Systems, 1999, 2, p. 8-13.

http://www.tiger.edu.pl/kolodko/artykuly/99_2.pdf

64. 《从市场改革到市场经济转轨》《前苏东国家早期经济改革的经验教训》(Lessons from Early Economic Reforms of the Former Soviet Union and Eastern Europe) (Chinese Economic Research Institute of China Reform Foundation), Proceedings of International Symposium, August 1997, p. 35-49.

http://www.tiger.edu.pl/kolodko/artykuly/1997_8.pdf

Author's Publications on China in the English Language

» *The Quest for Development Success*: *Bridging Theoretical Reasoning with Economic Practice* (2021), Lexington Books, - Rowman & Littlefield, Lanham-Boulder-New York – London.

» "Some Reflections on China and Globalization", in: *TIGER Working Paper Series*, 145(March), Transformation, Integration and Globalization Economic Research, Tiger, Kozminski University, Warsaw.
http://www.tiger.edu.pl/publikacje/working.htm

» *Economics and Politics of the Great Change*: *Mikhail Gorbachev versus Deng Xiaoping*, "Kwartalnik Nauk o Przedsiębiorstwie" (2021), No. 1 (58).

» "The Great Chinese Transformation: from the Third to the First World", *Acta Oeconomica* (2020), Vol. 70, Special Issue, p. 71-83.
https://akjournals.com/view/journals/032/70/S/article-p71.xml

» "Chinism and the Future of the World", *Communist and Post-Communist Studies* (2020), Vol. 53, No. 4, p. 260-279.
https://doi.org/10.1525/j.postcomstud.2020.53.4.260

» *China and the Future of Globalization*: *The Political Economy of China's Rise* (2020). , I.B. Tauris Bloomsbury, London – New York, p. XII + 188.

» "Better paths needed to help shape the future", *China Daily* (2020), April 28.
http://tiger.edu.pl/CHINA%20DAILY_28.04.2020.pdf

» *Chinism and the future of globalisation* (2020), RI-DOC, Research Institute Dialogue of Civilizations, Meet in Mitte Lecture, Berlin, February 24

» "Chinese Economy at the Era of Globalization", *Academics* (2019), No. 7 (254), July, p. 178-187.

» "Socialism, Capitalism, or Chinism?", *Communist and Post-Communist Studies* (2018), Vol. 51, Issue 4, p. 285-298.

» "Chinese Economy at the Era of Globalization", in: *The Contours of the Future in the Context of the World's Cultural Development* (2018), St. Petersburg University of the Humanities and Social Sciences, St. Petersburg, p. 75-80.

» "Economic expansion of China: determinants, perspectives, limits", *Economic and Regional Studies* (2018), Vol. 11, No. 1, p. 7-19.

» "Capitalism, Socialism or Chinism?", *EconoMonitor* (2018), January
https://www.themaven.net/economonitor/asia/capitalism-socialism-or-chinism-uhB-e4jtfUyQ9TZEBRGyCw?full=1

» "Will China Save the World?", *Economonitor* (2017), May 24
http://www.economonitor.com/blog/2017/05/will-china-save-the-world/

» "What China's Leaders Could Learn From Poland", *Bloomberg* (2016), April 22.
http://www.bloomberg.com/news/articles/2016-04-21/as-china-mulls-reforms-champion-of-polish-model-flags-lessons

» "On China and the world of the future", *Hurriyet Daily News* (2016), April 6, p. A2.

» "Institutions, Policies and Development", in: *Public Service Systems in China: Relationship Between the Central and Local Governments* (2006), Collection of Papers, China Institute for Reform and Development (CIRD), Haikou, Hainan (China), October 28-29, p. 1-29.

» "Introductory remarks", in: Justin Yifu Lin, *Lessons of China's Transition from a Planned Economy to a Market Economy* (2004), Distinguished Lectures Series, No. 16, Leon Kozminski Academy of Entrepreneurship and Management (WSPiZ), Warsaw, p. 1-7.
http://www.tiger.edu.pl/publikacje/dist/lin.pdf

About the Author

A key architect of Polish economic reforms, professor Grzegorz W. Kolodko – the laureate of the 2020 Special Book Award of China – is a key architect of Polish economic reforms, renowned academic, public intellectual and politician, author of the New Pragmatism – original paradigmatic and heterodox theory of economics and economic policy addressing the civilizational challenges and transformation of economic systems. He is the world's most quoted Polish economist.

He is also the Member of the European Academy of Arts, Sciences, and Humanities, Doctor *Honoris Causa* and Honorary Professor of a dozen foreign universities, including three in China; author of numerous books and research papers published in 26 languages, including international bestseller *Truth, Errors, and Lies: Politics and Economics in a Volatile World* nominated for the William Harrington Award "for an outstanding book that demonstrates how scholarship can be used in the struggle for a better world", and *China and the Future of Globalization: Political Economy of China's Rise* nominated the *Financial Times* Summer 2020 book.

He is the participant in the historical Polish "Round Table", which led to the first post-communist government in Central and Eastern Europe. As Deputy Prime Minister and Minister of Finance (1994-1997) he led Poland to the Organization for Economic Cooperation and Development, OECD. Holding the same positions in 2002-2003 he played important role in Poland's integration with the European Union.

He is the Founding Director of TIGER – Transformation, Integration and Globalization Economic Research at Kozminski University in Warsaw – and Distinguished Professor at Belt and Road School at Beijing Normal University and International Adviser to the Center for China and Globalization, CCG.

He is at the same time the marathon runner (50 finished runs, including Beijing), photographer and globetrotter who's explored 170 countries and visited Antarctica.